Praise for Read. Write. Reflect.

"In *Read. Write. Reflect.*, Monica Bhide's gentle, lyrical voice guides you to a more inspired level of creativity. I recommend this encouraging guide for any creative soul that needs constant or occasional nurturing."

**Sandra Beckwith, author and publisher,
BuildBookBuzz.com**

"To know Monica Bhide is to be inspired. She is a thought leader not only in the culinary world, but for those seeking a deeper connection with their passion and their purpose. Through this lovely collection of essays and prompts, Monica will light the kindest of fires under anyone – artist, scientist, wanderer – while creating a safe space to be more intentional. I highly recommend reading, savoring and putting the wisdom within to use!"

Casey Benedict, president, Kitchen PLAY

"*Read. Write. Reflect.* is the perfect blend of creative inspiration and pragmatic action. It breaks past the fears that hamper most writers, empowering you to find a renewed sense of clarity and purpose in your writing. If you feel stuck in your writing, *Read. Write. Reflect.* will help you get unstuck."

Dan Blank, author of Be the Gateway

"*Read. Write. Reflect.* is a refreshing insight into the writing process, and it is a process. Monica brings a truly reflective lens to the work of being a creative. It's like having a very wise voice in your ear, asking you the questions that keep you moving forward, even when the going gets tough. It should be on your must-read list."

Andrea King Collier, journalist, essayist, and author

"I define 'success' as having your life on your terms. And the single most valuable success lesson that I continue to learn, grow and literally profit from is SLOWING DOWN. In the instruction manual Monica includes in this masterpiece, she reminds us of the need to do precisely that – slow down enough to be present with what is, so that we can work creatively and masterfully with that. I just love the short, poignant stories and the collection of suggested listening and reading references are as impressive as it gets. Thank you, Monica Bhide, sincerely, for slowing down enough to make the time to create this collection, this creativity workbook. I will use it as a daily source of inspiration."

Chris Dorris, Mental Toughness speaker/author/coach

"Aspiring writers, or artists of any stripe, would do well to heed the excellent advice in Monica Bhide's *Read. Write. Reflect.* If nothing else, the concept of 'Timeboxed Whining' will stay with me for life!"

Sarah Knight, internationally bestselling author of
The Life-Changing Magic of Not Giving a F*ck *and*
Get Your Shit Together

"Like a Tiffany diamond, Monica Bhide's *Read. Write. Reflect.* has many facets – each brilliant and each complements the other to create a joyous mental illumination.

Giving advice is the easiest thing to do but it takes genius to do it in a way that is motivating, energizing and inspiring.

From writing food recipes the author has created a gem of a recipe for success and a blueprint for living a life that you can be proud of. To be honest, this is very hard work but the bitter pills have been made palatable, even delicious, through her unique charm, wit and humor.

You can read the nuggets of wisdom in *Read. Write. Reflect.* and be entertained or you can take them to heart, put them into practice and transform yourself and your life. The ball or the book is in your court now!"

Deepak Sethi, CEO, Organic Leadership

Read. Write. Reflect.

Inspiration for Creative Minds

Monica Bhide

Foreword by Therese Walsh, Writer Unboxed

Cover photo by Simi Jois

Cover image by Simi Jois, Copyright © 2017
Formatting by Polgarus Studio

Bodes Well Publishing
Please contact publisher@bodeswellpublishing.com about special discounts for bulk purchases.

Disclaimer

This book is designed to provide information and motivation to our readers. The publisher and author are not engaged to render any type of psychological, legal, or any other kind of professional advice. No warranties or guarantees are expressed or implied by the publisher or the author. Neither the publisher nor the individual author shall be liable for any physical, psychological, emotional, financial, or commercial damages, including, but not limited to, special, incidental, consequential, or other damages.

Contents

Foreword

If being at the helm of Writer Unboxed for the last eleven years has taught me anything at all, it's that *Read. Write. Reflect.* is exactly the sort of fuel writers crave most.

It's positive and empowering.

The pages of Monica Bhide's book are loaded with positive, empowering, accessible wisdom for writers. But reading this book is not a passive undertaking, as Monica will also ask you to turn inward to unearth your own wisdom. The power of raising up your own stories and considering their specific details cannot be underestimated, for in asking you to take part in dozens of key exercises, Monica will awaken something that is uniquely your own – the DNA, as it were, of your own motivation.

It's personal and potent, and it's this book's true muscle.

Read. Write. Reflect. will inspire you to work through roadblocks, make commitments to yourself in order to move past them, and challenge yourself with still more difficult goals along the way. You will push aside old excuses and fears, and recall the power of stillness, grace, gratitude, and faith. You will arm yourself with new perspectives, and feel newly empowered to let go of the things that aren't working for you while embracing those things that are. You will recommit, not only to your work but also to yourself. You will face the mirror when Monica suggests you may be stalled because your perception about your skillset – and your very mindset – has been warped, and not because you aren't capable of completing the work.

In the spirit of Monica's book, I'd like to tell you a brief story.

One day, a woman stepped outside after a long rain. The sun shone, but rather than notice its warmth she focused on the thick mud bed that was once her garden. Around her, the faces of her favorite flowers drooped, heavy with earth. She had a sense of what needed to be done: Clean those flowers, prune away the death in order to save what could be saved. But instead of doing any of that, she lay with them in their bed of mud, her head low and face drooped.

The season continued. More rain came, and with it more mud, and yet the woman remained in place. Her family tried to coax her inside, but she would not budge.

"Just try," they would say. "You can stand," they would say.

But she would not. And though her family loved her, though they brought her food and blankets, and tugged at her arms, and told her stories, and encouraged her as much as they were able, the woman's situation was not sustainable, and soon she passed, sadly, with the season.

You might think her garden died with her, but it did not. Her flowers returned the next spring, their roots progressing downward and stems ever upward, their faces raised toward the sun.

Pinned to the top of my Twitter account is the following:

"Move, every day. Not just physically, but mentally. Don't settle. Strive."

Movement for writers means, naturally, progress on the page: one word in front of the other. Sometimes those words come quickly – a writer's sprint. Most often those words crawl. That's natural. What's important is that we keep on keeping on.

Progress is essential for we the people. Our worst choice is almost always sustained *in*action – physical and intellectual. Monica's book highlights those important human traits that can keep us from ever lying down in the mud. They are what we need not only to keep on keeping on, but to evolve into better, healthier writers. Writers who persevere, who finish. Writers who succeed.

Write on.

Therese Walsh
Editorial Director, *Writer Unboxed*
Author, *The Moon Sisters* and *The Last Will of Moira Leahy*
Editor, *Author in Progress*

Introduction

As a writer, I often look for inspiration in my most quiet times, but instead find it during the craziest/most mundane/silliest moments! These everyday moments not only inspire me but also help me find solutions to my own writer's block, help me feel more present in the now. They make me slow down and just focus on the pure pleasure of life. I liken these moments to meditation. Typically, meditation is a time of calmness, but for me these moments are times that have made me reflect, made my mind wander a bit, and forced me to just be with no judgments or failure or success.

It was during one of these insane moments, inspired and motivated by my friend Casey Benedict, that I decided to run a free program on my website. The program, titled *Powered by Hope,* was designed to inspire and motivate writers and artists to find their own moments (crazy or not) to reflect. The response was spectacular and beyond my wildest dreams! Everyone who subscribed to it, from far and wide, loved it. The comments ranged from motivating to inspiring to lifesaving. I would get emails from subscribers every week telling me what worked, which stories they loved and identified with, and how the simple nuggets helped them!

Encouraged by the feedback I received from my subscribers, I have pulled together my crazy moments—professionally referred to as bite-sized essays—featured in the *Powered by Hope* program and created this little book for you. This book, *Read. Write. Reflect.,* is intended to provide fun, motivation, and perhaps even some gentle self-reflection. I have taught writing classes all over the world, I have mentored aspiring and published writers, and I have learned from all of them. And the biggest lesson I have learned is that almost all of us face the same sorts of creative blocks. It is my hope that this book will help you deal with these blocks.

The moments showcased in this book focus on common fears, and provide us with a different viewing lens for the problem. Perspective, as they say, is everything—and changing it can help change your life. I am hopeful that the moments I have shared will provide you with a fresh, uplifting perspective.

The essays are meant to be a guide, sort of like a friend talking to you about how you would react in a situation or how a situation would affect you. These are *not* meant to be a replacement for medical, financial, legal, or any other professional advice. They are meant to feed your creative soul!

I hope you will enjoy this short book, and I look forward to hearing about your crazy moments! Connect with me on my website, MonicaBhide.com.

How to Use This Book

This interactive program is intended to inspire and motivate. It follows the motto: "Be led by your hopes, not your fears." These words take inspiration from the great Nelson Mandela's life, path, and words, "May your choices reflect your hopes, not your fears." To be led by faith in your own abilities and not fear of the future or fear of the unknown or all the other fears that haunt all of us. I strongly believe that those who succeed are the ones who stand up to their inner demons and do not let the demons win. They outlast their fears and create a positive life for themselves.

Read any essay in this book at your leisure, preferably in the morning. This book is not intended to be a step-by-step program but rather a self-reflection tool. The essays are intentionally short and will be quick to read; the messages are short and concise. Each essay asks questions. Mull over the questions for a few minutes. If nothing comes to you, give yourself more time to think. We are so used to moving fast that we forget to just give ourselves some space to think and digest. When you are ready, answer the questions provided in the *Write* section of each essay.

Once you have written your responses, then move on to the

Reflect section for each essay. I provide additional reading recommendations, podcasts, and other creative tools in that section. And, most importantly, that section gives you a place to make a commitment to yourself and decide what one piece of advice/truth/to-do you are going to carry forward with you. It could be as simple as committing yourself to express more gratitude or as complicated as creating detailed work plans for your projects. Even if you decide to do nothing, that is a decision! Here is the deal: Committing is a choice. This section is meant to enable you to choose, decide on, and make the changes that will help *you* feed your creative spirit.

Here's to your creative success!

BE STILL

When my son was about five, I took him for a swimming lesson. I never learned how to swim and so I was determined to make sure that my kids did. He went into the water with his teacher and began to flap his arms wildly and, yes, panic. The teacher, kind as ever, kept saying, "Son, in order to make this work, you have to slow down. You have to learn to love the water and it will love you back. Just calm down and just be still. You have to learn to understand the water, understand how it behaves before you can control it. You have to calm down."

Well, my son continued to struggle for a bit and the teacher continued to talk as calmly as he could. The lesson ended with a lot of tears and a huge tantrum of never wanting to go in the water again.

When it was time for the next lesson, my son was adamant about not wanting to go. He hated the water, hated the teacher, he said. But I knew it was fear that was taking over. We decided he would go and do nothing, just stand still in the water, and if that was too much then we would leave.

As he got into the pool that day, I stood quietly and watched. The instructor stood with him and they both just stared into the water. There was so much noise around them as other kids and families played, swam, and horsed around. Then the instructor turned to my son and said, "You know that you can lie on top of the water and if you are really still, you will float!"

My son stopped struggling and the instructor laid him flat on his back. The instructor had his arms under my son's back. Once the little boy was floating, the instructor removed his hands and my son floated without flailing, without fighting, without failing.

There is power in stillness. Sometimes, when everything is fighting back, it is time to be quiet, to be still, to learn to float.

The stillness, I have learned, is where the magic happens.

Write

Your thoughts:

Do you agree? Do you make time to be still? Should you?

_____

_____

_____

_____

_____

_____

_____

_____

_____

_____

_____

_____

_____

_____

_____

Reflect

Based on your answers to the previous questions, what one thing are you willing to commit to that will feed your creative soul? Now think about it and use the space below to make a commitment to yourself. Just one small thing. You can do it! Come on!

I commit ...

_____

_____

_____

_____

_____

_____

_____

_____

_____

Additional recommendations:

 Search for meditation podcasts and see which one appeals to you. I enjoy listening to just the sound of waves when I work. It helps me stay still. (YouTube has some great relaxing wave sounds.)

 Read *Still Writing: The Perils and Pleasures of a Creative Life* by Dani Shapiro. The book offers terrific insight into the creative life.

BELIEVE

Several years ago, I started a physical, cardboard vision board. You have heard of these things, right? A board where you post your goals, your dreams, your hopes. You put the board up where you can see it each day, and then the idea is that the Universe helps you achieve your dreams by helping you focus your efforts on your highly visible and visual goals.

Initially, nothing happened with my vision board. I would post a lot of stuff on it and then try to work toward the goals, but it never resulted in anything. An example: I posted the picture of one of my dream magazines and wrote under it "by Monica Bhide"—implying, of course, that I wanted a byline in the magazine. I faithfully sent out queries to several editors at the magazine and gained a respectable email pile of rejections. I began losing faith. I noticed this was happening in most of the areas on the vision board.

What was I not doing right? I began to read up about vision boards and goals and tried desperately to find out what I was doing wrong. I had the goals, I was working toward them—so why was I not achieving anything other than aggravation and frustration?

Sometimes the answer is so simple. Oprah has "Aha" moments in her magazine; I had a "Duh" moment and realized what had happened. I had NO faith, none at all, that any of the goals I had set for myself were achievable. I reread some of the queries I had sent—they sounded more like apologies than notes from a seasoned writer. I have to tell you, it was eye-opening.

To achieve a goal that you set for yourself, you must believe that you can do it. If you don't believe in yourself, not only will you not achieve the goal, but no one else will believe in you, either. Wasn't it Henry Ford who said something to the effect of: "If you think you can or you think you can't, you are right"?

Write

Your thoughts:

Do you believe you can accomplish your goals? Do you believe in your vision? Why? Why not? What is the one big thing holding you back? How do you intend to tackle it? (Yes, you can. I don't believe there is anything you cannot tackle one small step at a time.)

Reflect

Based on your answers to the previous questions, what one thing are you willing to commit to that will feed your creative soul? Now think about it and use the space below to make a commitment to yourself. Just one small thing. You can do it! Come on!

I promise ...

_____

_____

_____

_____

_____

_____

_____

_____

_____

_____

Additional recommendations:

 Listen to podcasts on creating the life you want. I love listening to *On Being* by Krista Tippett.

There are hundreds of books on creating a vision board and yes, they will all tell you pretty much the same thing. I do recommend you read one of them, but then read more books on *people in your field who have succeeded*. I loved Marcia Layton Turner's book *The Complete Idiot's Guide to Vision Boards.*

FOCUS

A few years ago, I found myself in a difficult spot. I was surrounded by noise; it seemed I needed more of everything, and yet nothing that I got made me happy. I recall feeling overwhelmed and yet very empty at the same time. It was a classic situation of "water, water everywhere."

In a feeble attempt to clear my head, I began to clean my sons' toy room. As I was putting away their books and toys, I found a bunch of Indian comic books lying around. I picked up the one about Arjuna, a talented prince in Hindu mythology. My younger son is named after this brave warrior prince, and I thought perhaps I could read my son the story that night.

Turns out the lesson applied to me more than it applied to my son. The story opens with a teacher, Guru Dronacharya, training a group of royal Indian princes, the Pandava brothers, in the art and skill of archery. The guru tied a fish to the branch of a tree. He then called all the warriors and said to them, "See that bowl of oil placed below the fish? I want you to aim your arrow at the fish's eye, while looking only at its reflection in the oil below."

"Oh, this will be easy," the princes said out loud.

The oldest prince, Yudhistra, came first, ready with his bow and arrow, and the guru asked, "What do you see?" He answered, "I see the fish, the leaves . . ."

The guru shook his head. "You are not ready. Move on."

The next prince came up and the guru asked him the same question. He responded that he saw the sky in the bowl of oil. He was asked to move on.

The third one saw the fish, the branches, and fruit. The fourth saw the leaves and the oil. They were both asked to step aside.

Finally, it was Prince Arjuna's turn. "What do you see?" asked the guru.

"I see the eye of the fish." The guru smiled and gave Prince Arjuna the order to shoot. The ace archer's arrow pierced the eye of the fish.

The story hit home for me. I was focused on the sky, the branches, the numbers, the followers, the echo of praise gone by and the hollowness of the feared future—when what I needed to do was focus on the moment at hand and what it demanded of me. For me that meant working on a dream writing project.

Write

Your thoughts:

What is your moment at hand? Are you focused on the sky, the leaves, the fish? What do you need to be focused on? What is your "eye of the fish"?

_____

_____

_____

_____

_____

_____

_____

_____

_____

_____

_____

_____

_____

_____

Reflect

Based on your answers to the previous questions, what one thing are you willing to commit to that will feed your creative soul? Now think about it and use the space below to make a commitment to yourself. Just one small thing. You can do it! Come on!

I will focus on ...

_____

_____

_____

_____

_____

_____

_____

_____

_____

Additional recommendations:

 Tim Ferriss has a terrific podcast and I highly recommend it. He does interesting and practical shows on productivity and focus. Well worth your time!

 Read Daniel Goleman's *Focus: The Hidden Driver of Excellence.*

CHOICE

My father lives in New Delhi, India. For the past ten years or so, each month without fail he has snail-mailed me packages filled with clippings from newspapers and magazines. When he first started sending them, they were filled with food news from local Delhi papers. The stories varied from being about the newest restaurant to open in Delhi, to the health benefits of drinking tea, to how to eat like a maharaja.

About five years ago, I remember, a package came, just as the one before it and the one before that. I remember one small clipping—, it was a cartoon about six inches by six inches. The cartoon showed an old man sitting on a stone talking to a young child.

The child says, "Grandfather, there are two wolves knocking at my door. One is the wolf of abundance, pleasure, blessings, generosity, wealth, and bounty. And the other one is the wolf of anxiety, grief, sadness, lack of abundance, stress, and pressure."

The child continues, "They are both knocking hard, Grandfather. Please tell me who will come in? Who will win and gain entry into my home?

The grandfather answers, "Whichever one you feed."

The cartoon struck a chord. It is so easy to let in the stress. At the time I received this package, I had been having a hard time finding work and created all the excuses in the world about why I would never be successful. My negativity was fulfilled by the Universe; misery attracted misery.

After seeing the cartoon, I began to focus on what I could do well, and on doing that instead of worrying. I chose which wolf I was feeding.

Success, abundance, prosperity, love, [insert your own need] come from what we choose to let inside our minds and then let out as actions and thoughts. The key word here is *choice*. There's no way our lives are easy. Things are rough with most everyone I know, but how we react, whom we let in the door, is our choice.

Write

Your thoughts:

So tell me: Who is knocking on your door these days, and which wolf are you going to feed?

_____

_____

_____

_____

_____

_____

_____

_____

_____

_____

_____

_____

_____

Reflect

Based on your answers to the previous questions, what one thing are you willing to commit to that will feed your creative soul? Now think about it and use the space below to make a commitment to yourself. Just one small thing. You can do it! Come on!

I will ...

_____

_____

_____

_____

_____

_____

_____

_____

Additional recommendations:

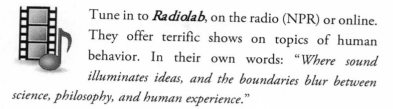 Tune in to **Radiolab**, on the radio (NPR) or online. They offer terrific shows on topics of human behavior. In their own words: "*Where sound illuminates ideas, and the boundaries blur between science, philosophy, and human experience.*"

Check out the **Zen Habits: Breathe** newsletter (zenhabits.net). Leo Babauta always offers simple yet effective techniques for stillness, focus, and commitment—among other things.

Read

FILTER

When I was in engineering college, we studied the concept of GIGO: Garbage In/Garbage Out. Basically it taught us that the computer wasn't capable of distinguishing bad input from good input; it would process it all and if the input was illogical/silly/useless, the output would be useless as well.

I find this concept works well with life, too. I used to work with the TV running in the background, mostly on the news channel. By the end of the day, I would find myself really cranky and, frankly, very depressed. I realized that while I was not consciously listening to the TV, some part of my brain was taking in all the bad news *constantly*. Same applied for what I read—I read gossip sections of magazines, and newspapers filled with news of every disaster known to man. And watched the nightly news broadcasting all that was bad in the world. Now, I am not saying that we should not watch the news or consume information; all I am saying is that I had to be careful what I was consuming, and how much. I was taking in all bad and nothing good. There was no balance.

Now I try to listen to classical music as I work. It makes the room and my brain feel more at peace. I watch the news, but only once a day. I read the papers, but try not to go into the details of gory murder stories. And each night, I end my day with reading something inspiring, something that fills my mind with possibilities, something that informs rather than scares. After all: Garbage In, Garbage Out.

Your thoughts:

How do you handle all the information coming your way? How do you filter it? Are you taking in any inspiring, motivating works? If not, how do you plan to change that?

_____

_____

_____

_____

_____

_____

_____

_____

_____

_____

_____

_____

Reflect

Based on your answers to the previous questions, what one thing are you willing to commit to that will feed your creative soul? Now think about it and use the space below to make a commitment to yourself. Just one small thing. You can do it! Come on!

I commit ...

_____

_____

_____

_____

_____

_____

_____

_____

Additional recommendations:

 Listen to your favorite instrumental music instead of the sounds of 24-hour news or pretty much anything that is negative. I am not saying you should NOT listen to the news—just not all the time. Add a few minutes into your day to listen to an inspirational podcast, a piece of music that makes you want to dance, or just the sounds of nature. Try the wonderful *The Daily Boost* podcast, or listen to one of the many **TED Talks**.

 I really enjoyed Daniel J. Levitin's *The Organized Mind*, a book that teaches us how to stay organized and focused in the era of information overload.

INSPIRE

As many parents will attest, we do a lot of waiting. I wait at soccer practice, I wait in the car pool line, I wait at play dates. My waiting time is supposed to be my learning time—I read, catch up on my podcasts—but mostly I spend it staring into space.

On one such waiting occasion, I was standing in a harshly lit corridor at the local community center, waiting for my son to come out of his class. It felt like I was in, quite possibly, one of the most boring spots on earth. I had forgotten to bring a book and the place did not have WiFi, so I was just standing there, wondering what to do.

Then I heard it: loud, blaring music coming from the end of the corridor. I turned to see a young man place a stereo on the ground, and then he began to dance. From the grace of his movements, I could tell he was trained. His movements were fluid, his body seemed to glide through the air, his hands moved around with practiced accuracy and with the gentleness of a bud opening to the world. As mesmerized as I was with his dancing, what caught my eye was his face. He seemed to be one with his dance, with his music. He smiled as he danced, his expressions changed as the beats changed.

He was so absorbed in his dance and in the music, he did not even see my son and his friends who had gathered around me to watch him. He just danced, almost in a trance. He glowed. The kids went up to him after he finished dancing and applauded loudly. He was the local dance instructor and now had so many new kids who wanted to sign up for his class after seeing him dance.

As we drove home, I kept thinking about how lucky the dancer was to reach that state—"dance like no one is watching"—and how it resulted in more students for him. Passion inspires.

Write

Your thoughts:

What are you passionate about? Would you ever dance like no one is watching? Why? Why not?

_____

_____

_____

_____

_____

_____

_____

_____

_____

_____

_____

_____

_____

Reflect

Based on your answers to the previous questions, what one thing are you willing to commit to that will feed your creative soul? Now think about it and use the space below to make a commitment to yourself. Just one small thing. You can do it! Come on!

My passion...

_____

_____

_____

_____

_____

_____

_____

_____

Additional recommendations:

 This recommendation may seem a little strange, but: watch movies or documentaries with a sports theme. These always inspire me and fill me with energy! YouTube has a great collection of "**best motivational speeches**." Some of these are best moments from sports movies.

 Read a biography of someone whom you have long admired—Steve Jobs, Stephen King, Andre Agassi, Oprah Winfrey . . . pick one! Commit to reading it and learning from it.

TENACITY

I have a dear friend who is an excellent writer. She writes, primarily, for herself. She is very talented but the world will never see her talent. It makes me sad to even write this. Why won't the world see it? You see, my friend uses every excuse in the book not to send her work to an editor or an agent. I have heard all these over the decades I have known her:

It is not ready yet. I am not good enough. They will hate it. It is Sunday and I want to wait till Monday [the Monday that never comes]. No one understands my style of writing. I just don't have the strength to finish this. My muse is not cooperating. The manuscript sucks.

And plenty more. I know them all by heart. I am not trying to say that her fears are not real. They are. To her, they are truly scary and are holding her back from what could be a Pulitzer. She really is that good. All of us have our own crosses to bear, and this is hers. I have tried to reason with her, to get mad at her, to yell, to be kind, to say that I will secretly mail her manuscript out to someone—but she won't listen. And I am sad to say that several years ago, she stopped writing. Totally stopped. Fear won over talent.

Now let's compare her with a blogger friend of mine. When she started, she did not have a word to her name. No bylines. Nothing. But she did not use any of the excuses above. Instead, she quietly started a blog and began posting her thoughts and recipes. It grew. She sent the link to editors to make them notice her work. They gave her work. Her workload—and paycheck—grew. She has achieved something that people a TON more talented than she is have not: She has been able to put herself out there and make her dream a reality.

There is one critical difference between Friend 1 (the novelist who will not publish) and Friend 2 (the food blogger who is making a name for herself): Friend 2 chose herself. Friend 1 is still waiting to be the chosen one.

This is critical. As creative people, we are always waiting for some editor/producer/etc. to pick us. But I take a lesson from Friend 2 who is doing it so well: put myself out there. The days I fail teach me a lot more than the days on which I succeed. There are very few chosen ones. The rest of us have to make our own luck.

Write

Your thoughts:

What are you going to do to make your own luck? Starting tomorrow, what is the one thing you know you can do that will move you toward the direction of your dreams?

_____

_____

_____

_____

_____

_____

_____

_____

_____

_____

_____

_____

Reflect

Based on your answers to the previous questions, what one thing are you willing to commit to that will feed your creative soul? Now think about it and use the space below to make a commitment to yourself. Just one small thing. You can do it! Come on!

I commit ...

_____

_____

_____

_____

_____

_____

_____

_____

_____

Additional recommendations:

 Listen to *The Partially Examined Life*. There is a new podcast I am going to listen to, and maybe you can try it as well: *The Art of Charm*.

 Read Austin Kleon's *Show Your Work!* or *Steal Like an Artist*. Excellent, short reads.

LAUGH

When my older son was two years old, he loved doing things by himself. I remember one day he was trying to put his seat belt on, but it was too tight. Finally, he called to me, "Mama, can you help, this belt is too tight." Of course, I was thrilled to help and rushed over and loosened his belt. Happy and comfortable now in his car seat, he looked at me ever so sweetly and said, "Mama, you are the best loser ever!" You know, because I had loosened his belt.

Each time something goes wrong, I remind myself that I am already the best loser ever—how much worse can it get?

Your thoughts:

What funny stories from your life get you through tough days? Do you feel like you laugh enough? As a child, what was the funniest thing you ever heard? What was the funniest thing you ever said?

_____

_____

_____

_____

_____

_____

_____

_____

_____

_____

_____

_____

Reflect

Based on your answers to the previous questions, what one thing are you willing to commit to that will feed your creative soul? Now think about it and use the space below to make a commitment to yourself. Just one small thing. You can do it! Come on!

I promise ...

_____

_____

_____

_____

_____

_____

_____

_____

_____

Additional recommendations:

There are as many studies out there about the health benefits of laughter as there are birds in the sky—so why don't we laugh more? Watch your favorite funny movie, download a funny podcast, watch funny baby videos on YouTube. I love Robin Williams, and his funny movies always make me smile.

Did you know there is a *Laughter Is the Best Medicine Coloring Book*? How about reading *The Laughing Cure* by Brian King? Or *The Healing Power of Humor* by Allen Klein? Try Mindy Kaling's *Is Everyone Hanging Out Without Me?* Or anything by **Erma Bombeck**.

PERSISTENCE

A key factor in any endeavor is to pursue it like there is no tomorrow. Sounds simplistic? Common sense? Well—it is. It is as simple as that. I have met many people in this world with a lot of talent who can really talk a good talk. But I haven't seen their bylines, their terrific companies, their great products, or read the great American novel that they want to publish. Why not? They have no time, can't create the time, or have some other excuse. I know all their excuses and reasons because I have personally used almost every single excuse in the book about why I was not following my dream. I paid lip service to my dream, saying that I would do it all—someday.

If I was going to make my dream come true, I had to *do*, not say.

I began to print sayings on action and hung them on my wall. Post-it notes with "Do, do do" began to cover parts of my worktable.

It is easy to be persistent when all is going well. When the sun is shining outside your window and when your boss says he loves your work, or a friend calls to announce a new baby/promotion/etc. The real key is to be persistent when life seems to be going in the wrong direction and there seems to be nothing you can do.

I was on a plane recently and happened to glance at the *SkyMall* magazine. I saw the Destiny Tiles they are selling: "Watch your thoughts become words; watch your words become actions; watch your actions become habits; watch your habits become character; watch your character as it becomes your destiny."

It made me realize that persistence needs to be a character trait. But let me define persistence. It is not about following up on things, it is about following through. Persistence is about owning your intentions and not letting any outside force or the stronger inside force move you away from what you need to accomplish.

Write

Your thoughts:

How are you going to keep moving forward? The past offers only lessons; the future offers hope. But the key is to DO NOW. What are you going to do?

_____

_____

_____

_____

_____

_____

_____

_____

_____

_____

_____

_____

Reflect

Based on your answers to the previous questions, what one thing are you willing to commit to that will feed your creative soul? Now think about it and use the space below to make a commitment to yourself. Just one small thing. You can do it! Come on!

I will ...

_____

_____

_____

_____

_____

_____

_____

Additional recommendations:

 Okay, so this may sound silly but, in all seriousness, tune in to commercials that are created for sports like soccer. In 30 seconds or less, these commercials help us visualize persistence. If you prefer podcasts, I once again recommend **Tim Ferriss**.

 Read the biography of a historical figure whom you admire but don't know enough about. Read *Unbroken* by Laura Hillenbrand.

Read

EXPLORE

I debated titling this page: The Butt-Out Post. Well, clearly, better sense prevailed! But it is what I want to talk about this morning: getting our butts out of our chairs. This is really a big and, sadly, underperformed function that every creative person needs to focus on when pursuing a dream project. Especially when the project hits a snag, or there is a dull moment and you feel compelled to clean the bathrooms for the sixth time that day instead of dealing with the issues on your project.

When I coach writers who are unable to write, I always tell them to leave their writing space—at least for a while. Go out and explore. Pick up your favorite chocolate bar and head to the newest museum/bookstore/clothing store in your area—or even better, outside your area—and just spend some time looking around. It is a great way to nurture the writer side of you that is looking for new experiences to write about. Maybe while wandering the children's museum you notice the brand-new system installed in the bathroom to dry your hands. Or the poor way a cross mother handles her son. Or the fact that the entire menu being served at the museum cafeteria is now organic. I am making some of this up, but these are things you would have never known if you had not gone out. One point here: This is something to do on your own, not with a kid or friend in tow. You want to give your mind the ability to think and look for new things, not gossip about George Clooney's new movie or worry about your baby's diaper.

This exploring does something important: It frees your mind to focus on your problem without "worrying about it." Sounds crazy, I know, but this is the equivalent of *I was in the shower, and suddenly the answer hit me!*

Going out and exploring, finding new sources of inspiration, finding how big the world really is and how much we still have to learn is, in my opinion, a powerful antidote to repeated bathroom cleaning to avoid working on your dream project.

Write

Your thoughts:

Pick one new thing you will explore this week. Why would you like to explore that? Is there any place you have wanted to visit all your life? If you had a choice of three amazing places you could visit (and a limitless budget), which one would you choose and why?

_____

_____

_____

_____

_____

_____

_____

_____

_____

_____

Reflect

Based on your answers to the previous questions, what one thing are you willing to commit to that will feed your creative soul? Now think about it and use the space below to make a commitment to yourself. Just one small thing. You can do it! Come on!

I promise ...

Additional recommendations:

Try the *Zero to Travel* podcast—a very interesting listen. One thing I do on a regular basis is go to YouTube and watch a video of a city I have always wanted to visit. Watch **Anthony Bourdain**. Have a date with yourself at a bookstore and luxuriate in reviewing books about distant—or local!—places.

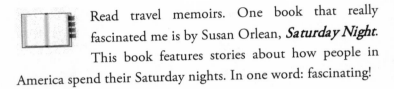

Read travel memoirs. One book that really fascinated me is by Susan Orlean, *Saturday Night*. This book features stories about how people in America spend their Saturday nights. In one word: fascinating!

TRY

Reality, I have learned, is in the mind of the thinker. Case in point: I don't know how to ride a bike. I never had the chance to learn when I was a child and then, after a certain point in my life, I felt like I was too old.

But then, one fine day I decided that I would post on Facebook that I wanted to learn how to ride a bike. Did people think I could do it? The answers were eye-opening. Those who knew how to ride a bike, or had learned at an older age, or were currently learning all said: *Yes, you can do it. Go ahead, get on. You will learn in no time.*

And then came the other messages: *Don't do it; if you fall, you will break your bones and they will take forever to heal.* And my favorite response: *What is the advantage to you to learn how to ride a bike? You already drive a car, so why bike? Also: You are too old, let it be.*

Instead of learning how to ride a bike, I learned something even more critical about human nature: If we think we can do something, we will likely try it and do it. But if we think we cannot, we may never even try.

Your thoughts:

What are you trying to do that is different or new to you? I think you can do it. Do you?

_____

_____

_____

_____

_____

_____

_____

_____

_____

_____

_____

_____

_____

Reflect

Based on your answers to the previous questions, what one thing are you willing to commit to that will feed your creative soul? Now think about it and use the space below to make a commitment to yourself. Just one small thing. You can do it! Come on!

I will ...

_____

_____

_____

_____

_____

_____

_____

_____

Additional recommendations:

I have been eagerly waiting to reach this point in this book so that I can recommend one of my most favorite podcasts of all times: *Invisibilia* on NPR. This terrific podcast is eye-opening. Don't believe me? Listen to the episode about the blind man who bikes. Trust me.

Read a book, a story, an essay, or anything that pleases you about the ONE thing you have committed to above. Read Twyla Tharp's *The Creative Habit.*

GIVE

Want something? They say to get what you really want, you need to give that out. Sounds a bit nuts, I know. But it works. I am surrounded by successful writers, chefs, and businesspeople, and you know what is the one common trait that I see in most of them? They are generous with their knowledge, their insights, and their experiences. In spite of having schedules that make them gallop around the world, in spite of being so busy that they can barely answer all their emails and phone calls, in spite of being pulled in seven directions at the same time, their response has always been: "How can I help?" Whether it is the answer to a simple recipe question or a "What am I doing with my life?" question; a "What makes a true brand?" query or a "Can you help me learn Mexican cuisine?" request—my questions are endless and their generosity trumps that endlessness. I think this works well for these folks because all the positive energy they put out, they get back in spades. Goodwill is contagious, and I always try to pay it forward.

A word of caution here: Goodwill is to be earned and is not something we are entitled to. I try to be respectful when asking. When people give me something, I try to be gracious, respectful and, above all, grateful.

And with giving? Give like no one is watching and everyone is in the know! A true giver gives without any sense of wanting anything back in return.

Write

Your thoughts:

What are you going to give? It doesn't have to be something materialistic—a kind word, a sweet note, a gentle hug all go a long way.

_____

_____

_____

_____

_____

_____

_____

_____

_____

_____

_____

_____

Reflect

Based on your answers to the previous question, what one thing are you willing to commit to that will feed your creative soul? Now think about it and use the space below to make a commitment to yourself. Just one small thing. You can do it! Come on!

I commit ...

_____

_____

_____

_____

_____

_____

_____

_____

_____

Additional recommendations:

 You are going to think that YouTube is paying me to mention them again and again! Let me assure you NO ONE is paying me anything to include links and books here! Please go to YouTube and search *Random Acts of Kindness*. You'll find some of the sweetest videos that are very uplifting. Follow the Humans of New York on Facebook and read some of the comments in the stories—people offering to help and support strangers. We live in a generous world (on most days!).

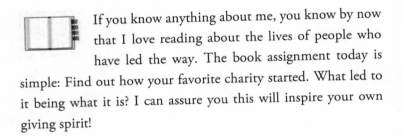 If you know anything about me, you know by now that I love reading about the lives of people who have led the way. The book assignment today is simple: Find out how your favorite charity started. What led to it being what it is? I can assure you this will inspire your own giving spirit!

Read

RECOGNIZE OPPORTUNITIES

You may have heard this story before; it has been making rounds on the internet. Please forgive me if I tell it once more.

> *A shoe company sends two salesmen to a small, remote village in Africa to check out the market there for shoes. The first one sends an email back: "Flying back tomorrow. There is no market here, no one wears shoes." The shoe company president reads the message and decides to call the young man back. The second salesman also sends an email, but his reads: "SEND MORE SHOES. No one here wears them so there is a huge market. Looks like I need to tell my wife I will be gone for a while." He got a promotion.*

If you think this story is internet legend or bogus, then go to Google and search out the story about the poor Indian man who created sanitary napkins. He found out that less than seven percent of Indian women used napkins. Others (mostly poor) just made do with small pieces of cloth. Instead of thinking "No one is doing it so there is no market," he spent years thinking, "93 percent market share!" He went to on to create jobs for millions of rural women who could now make these napkins at small local factories and use them.

These stories have made a huge impression on me. I tend to be the one with glass-half-empty syndrome, so now each time I am faced with a situation that looks less than positive, I remind myself of these stories.

Write

Your thoughts:

Are you on the lookout for opportunities? Think about one thing that happened today that could lead you to a new place—just one! If there are more, great! But start with one.

_____

_____

_____

_____

_____

_____

_____

_____

_____

_____

_____

_____

_____

_____

Reflect

Based on your answers to the previous question, what one thing are you willing to commit to that will feed your creative soul? Now think about it and use the space below to make a commitment to yourself. Just one small thing. You can do it! Come on!

I promise ...

_____

_____

_____

_____

_____

_____

_____

_____

Additional recommendations:

 Google the story about the Indian man and sanitary napkins! Why haven't I provided a link? Because technology is changing so fast, I am worried that links will be useless by the time this book comes out. Long live Google and Yahoo and Bing!

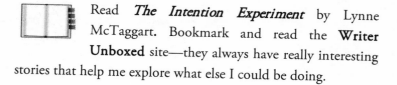 Read *The Intention Experiment* by Lynne McTaggart. Bookmark and read the **Writer Unboxed** site—they always have really interesting stories that help me explore what else I could be doing.

ATTITUDE

Ah, my favorite topic. I get regular emails from readers saying that I am too positive. This always makes me laugh. What is too positive? Would they rather read bad news? Would they rather I tell them all that is wrong with this world? Well, there are already so many people doing that and doing it well. Turn to any news channel, any news website, any blogger talking about politics or current events, and it is all there to read.

I try not to be Pollyanna, but I've found that if I am not positive, nothing that I am working on gets done. I make worrying about things an art form! I could worry about anything for any length of time—and sometimes I still do. But what I am finding more and more is that the worry does nothing except make me feel ill, both physically and mentally. What works better for me is to have a positive attitude with a focus that good things are coming, and I just have to *happily* keep working toward them. Whether or not the good things come then becomes moot because I am happy in my journey—and that is the point.

Write

Your thoughts:

Are you a glass-half-full or a glass-half-empty person? What works for you? Why? Is it enough to have a glass?

_____

_____

_____

_____

_____

_____

_____

_____

_____

_____

_____

_____

_____

Reflect

Based on your answers to the previous questions, what one thing are you willing to commit to that will feed your creative soul? Now think about it and use the space below to make a commitment to yourself. Just one small thing. You can do it! Come on!

I commit ...

_____

_____

_____

_____

_____

_____

_____

_____

_____

Additional recommendations:

 The podcast *A Quiet Mind* is worth tuning in to!

 Read the classic *The Power of Positive Thinking* by Dr. Norman Vincent Peale or *Three Feet from Gold* by Sharon L. Lechter and Greg S. Reid. The key to reading almost anything mentioned in my book is to read it not only as a reader, but also as a creative professional trying to gain insight into how to make your own creative work stronger. So read each book with a pen and a notebook in hand—make notes, write down inspiring ideas, and then put yourself to work by incorporating suggestions from the books into your own life. Does this sound like a lot of work? It really isn't!

GET OUT OF
YOUR COMFORT ZONE

My mother used to teach little kids. One year she taught them how to write a story about an object or an experience. If I remember correctly, the kids must have been in first grade, and the story consisted of five lines or so. The example she used was a story about a cow: "There was a cow in the meadow. The cow had four legs and a tail. The cow loved to eat the grass. . . ."

A few weeks later, Mom gave her class a test: "Your family took you on a picnic. Write a story about the picnic." I used to help her grade the tests—and now that the statute of limitations has passed, I can tell you I used to change some grades to make sure the borderline kids all passed.

Anyway, as I was reading the essays, it struck me that nine out of ten kids wrote: "My parents took me on a picnic. There we saw a cow. The cow was in the meadow. The cow had four legs and a tail. The cow loved to eat the grass. . . ."

I will never forget that. It taught me so many lessons, and one in particular that I want to discuss today: Creativity is about going out of your comfort zone. So many of us are comfortable with whatever our strength is—writing about preserves, or spices, or charcuterie—that we refuse to even tackle a new thing, thinking it will be too hard. We could never do it.

Write

Your thoughts:

So an important aspect of creativity is: Take the cow out of your picnic and try new things. What one new thing will you try this week?

_____

_____

_____

_____

_____

_____

_____

_____

_____

_____

_____

_____

_____

_____

Reflect

Based on your answers to the previous question, what one thing are you willing to commit to that will feed your creative soul? Now think about it and use the space below to make a commitment to yourself. Just one small thing. You can do it! Come on!

My new comfort zone ...

_____

_____

_____

_____

_____

_____

_____

Additional recommendations:

 Research and watch a movie that is in a genre you don't ever watch. Just one. See what you learn from it. Everything teaches us something. It may just be a bad movie—but then think about why! The idea is to stretch ourselves to experience new things.

 Read books on creativity. I love learning about how creative people use their time and progress. I loved Elizabeth Gilbert's *Big Magic.* Also try Brené Brown's *Daring Greatly.*

JUDGING

I was very opinionated as a child, often making strong remarks about other peoples' appearances. My father sometimes glared at me but never said anything. Then one day, he sat me down and told me a story that helped me understand why judging was so wrong. Of course, I was seven or so at the time, so that story had to be one that my little mind could understand, internalize, and own.

The maharaja of Alwar, of the princely Indian state of Rajasthan, used to love Rolls-Royce cars. This was in the early 1900s when Indian royalty adored buying these cars. Some even had their painters paint portraits of the cars, and a few had the cars decked out with jewels of all kinds. The story goes that this particular maharaja was visiting England and stopped into a Rolls-Royce showroom. He was dressed in a nondescript way and, as my father told me, he looked very plain. When he asked to see one of the cars, the salesman shooed him off, telling him that he could not afford the car and that he should leave.

The maharaja made a graceful exit. Upon returning to Alwar, he placed an order for seven Rolls-Royce cars. His condition was that that the salesman should come to deliver the cars.

When the cars arrived, the salesman set them all up outside the royal palace and waited to show them off to the maharaja.

The maharaja arrived, graceful as ever, and gave the order that the cars would be used to pick up the municipal garbage in the city of Alwar, and that no one in his family would ever buy that car again.

When I heard of the clerk who told Oprah Winfrey that she could not look at a bag because she probably could not afford it, it reminded me of the story of the maharaja.

I try hard not to judge. It is difficult sometimes, I admit, but now when I judge, I do it consciously and know that mine is a considered opinion and not just a bad call.

Write

Your thoughts:

What if you went one day without judging YOURSELF? What would that day look like? Good? Bad? Why?

_____

_____

_____

_____

_____

_____

_____

_____

_____

_____

_____

_____

_____

_____

Reflect

Based on your answers to the previous questions, what one thing are you willing to commit to that will feed your creative soul? Now think about it and use the space below to make a commitment to yourself. Just one small thing. You can do it! Come on!

I will ...

Additional recommendations:

 TED Talks – pretty much any one! But pick talks where they investigate how and why we judge people. There is an interesting one titled: "**Why I keep speaking up, even when people mock my accent.**"

So here is my challenge for you: Pick a public figure you really despise. Now read something they wrote or said. What new insights about them have you learned? The point here is not to like them or curse them, but to open your creative mind to look at things from a different perspective.

GRADES

My attempt at creative writing was not accepted in my high school. My English teacher, God bless her heart, never paid much attention to me except for the F (or what amounted to an F) she gave me once. I had written an essay on a spring morning, but it was not the "traditional spring morning" she wanted. She wanted an essay filled with springtime flowers, joy, the magnificence of Mother Nature. Instead, mine was on a spring in war-torn land—blood, guts, and no glory. She was not impressed. I managed to pass the class when the vice principal intervened and changed the grade, and I got an A. But she did not ever let me forget that F.

I have to admit that that failing grade stayed with me. I wanted to write, but something about that grade haunted me as I grew up. What if she was right? What if I was wrong? Was I a dark writer that no one would want to read?

Fast-forward twenty years. I quit my engineering job to become a food writer. Within 24 months of quitting I had stories in the *New York Times*, the *Washington Post*, *Food & Wine* and other prestigious magazines. I had found the strength to prove to her—and more importantly to myself—that I was not an F when it came to writing.

Write

Your thoughts:

Are you allowing a haunting memory to hold you back? I hope you will reconsider and let it go. No one can predict the future. Don't let someone's nasty words define yours. Ponder on this today. Please.

_____

_____

_____

_____

_____

_____

_____

_____

_____

_____

_____

Reflect

Based on your answers to the previous question, what one thing are you willing to commit to that will feed your creative soul? Now think about it and use the space below to make a commitment to yourself. Just one small thing. You can do it! Come on!

I let go ...

_____

_____

_____

_____

_____

_____

_____

_____

Additional recommendations:

There are so many podcasts on this, but for this section I am suggesting you skip the audio and focus on my suggestion below.

Get a blank notebook. Free your time for 30 minutes. Now, write down your life story as other people tell it. Then write down your story as YOU would tell it. Every day going forward, write down the story of your life as you WANT IT. Each time, add more detail. Write as many pages as you want. There is no limit. This journaling habit will help you clarify what demons are holding you back. You have to do this every day for at least 21 days. Trust the process. At the end of three weeks, you will have defined what you want to do with your life, seen the gaps that need to be filled—and can celebrate the wins you already have!

BOREDOM

Ah, boredom. When my kids are home for the summer, it takes about two hours for them to come running to me with a well-used complaint: "We have nothing to do, we are bored." What I have learned is that there is only one antidote for boredom: curiosity. I introduce them to things they know nothing about. Can they build me a kaleidoscope using my broken bangles? Can they learn how to plant mint? Can they learn to say six new words in Chinese? Yes, it keeps them busy, but it also makes them smarter. One summer, my older son learned card tricks by watching YouTube. He is quite an expert now!

Curiosity is one of the most important skills we can obtain, and yes, it can be learned. To nurture your curiosity, begin by always asking questions. You will be surprised at how much people don't know and how much they pretend to know! Go to places you would not normally visit: a hardware store, a bird sanctuary, a temple, a hospital cafeteria. Look around and let yourself absorb the atmosphere. In the great words of Pink Floyd: "All you touch and all you see, is all your life will ever be." So get out there and learn new things, ask loads of questions, and in your heart, be like the four-year-old who keeps wondering why the sky is blue and why leaves aren't.

I cooked an Indian meal for Chef José Andrés recently, and the minute he stepped into my kitchen, his questions started: "How did you use the coconut in this bean dish? What is the spice that I smell in this curry? What is the base for this curry?" Chef Carla Hall is super successful, cooking Southern meals around the country, and yet she called me one day to ask about Indian cuisine and how she could incorporate Indian spices in what she does.

Write

Your thoughts:

What are you curious about today?

_____

_____

_____

_____

_____

_____

_____

_____

_____

_____

_____

_____

_____

_____

_____

Reflect

Based on your answers to the previous question, what one thing are you willing to commit to that will feed your creative soul? Now think about it and use the space below to make a commitment to yourself. Just one small thing. You can do it! Come on!

I commit ...

_____

_____

_____

_____

_____

_____

_____

_____

_____

Additional recommendations:

Have you ever wondered about seemingly mundane things that you feel you should already know but don't? I am always trying to learn things which, by all accounts, I should understand. Ever wonder how the US Mint actually prints money? I once spent a day researching how cruise ships manage to serve so many meals so quickly. What really happens in the underground tunnels under Disney World? Pick a documentary like *How Things Work* and see what new things you learn!

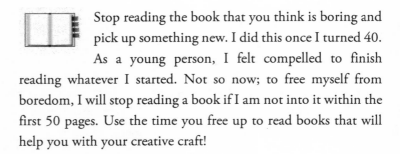

Stop reading the book that you think is boring and pick up something new. I did this once I turned 40. As a young person, I felt compelled to finish reading whatever I started. Not so now; to free myself from boredom, I will stop reading a book if I am not into it within the first 50 pages. Use the time you free up to read books that will help you with your creative craft!

Read

LOOKING INSIDE

One of the crazy fascinations I have, among many, is that I love to follow well-known people to see what makes them tick. What makes them do the things they do . . . what motivates them . . . what moves them . . . what inspires them. Yes, it is sort of like stalking them, but then I learn a lot.

I have started to do this to myself. If I set a goal now, I try to uncover my motivation behind it. Let's say I want to write a particular story. The question is always *why*—why should I write it, what is the value that I am providing, what is the difference this story is going to make if I tell it, or is it better told by someone else? When I find what is really motivating me, the obstacles no longer seem insurmountable because I have looked inside and found the *why me*.

I have tried to do this with my writing students who want to pursue their dreams of writing cookbooks. Why you? Why not someone else to write this book? What difference will it make if *you* write this book?

The answers are hard to come by and the question seems deceptively simple—but then we all know that looking inside is never easy!

Write

Your thoughts:

Are you working toward a dream goal? Have you thought about why?
Peel back the layers and think strong and hard about what is motivating
you to work on this project. The answers may surprise you.

_____

_____

_____

_____

_____

_____

_____

_____

_____

_____

_____

_____

Reflect

Based on your answers to the previous questions, what one thing are you willing to commit to that will feed your creative soul? Now think about it and use the space below to make a commitment to yourself. Just one small thing. You can do it! Come on!

I promise ...

_____

_____

_____

_____

_____

_____

_____

_____

Additional recommendations:

 For this exercise, interview someone whom you admire; it doesn't have to be a celebrity or any well-known personality. Pick a person who is passionate and ask them what drives them. How do they react to uncertainties, how do they face difficult situations, and what have they learned from their success? Use their answers to guide your own path.

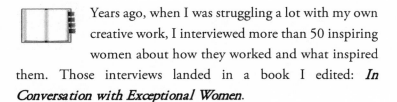 Years ago, when I was struggling a lot with my own creative work, I interviewed more than 50 inspiring women about how they worked and what inspired them. Those interviews landed in a book I edited: *In Conversation with Exceptional Women*.

Read

WORDS

I am going to get all new-agey on you here, so bear with me for a minute. As a writer I am acutely aware of the power of the written word, but the power of my own spoken words was not that important to me until I started seeing what was happening. I would always (half) jokingly introduce myself as the "starving writer." It was not really a joke, as I believed it in my heart. I believed that I was a starving writer, and that was how I showcased myself. Pretty soon, the people around me started believing it as well, and I would often be greeted with smiles of pity and hugs of sympathy.

I began to hate what I had created—the image of this pathetic, struggling writer. While parts of it were true, I truly loved what I did. I was passionate about writing, I *am* passionate about writing, I adore writing books, I find peace on the page. And yet, when I would talk to people, they would react to my "starving writer" image with offers of "real jobs" and sad nods.

Things had to change. I decided to introduce myself as an "aspiring writer." And can I tell you how much the reactions changed—I went from being pathetic to being interesting. People wanted to know what I was working on, if it was fun to write. Some even expressed that they had a secret desire to become an aspiring writer someday.

The power of words is strong. In my own head, when I went from starving to aspiring, I went from feeling like a victim to feeling like I had control and I could do something with my writing.

Write

Your thoughts:

How do you introduce yourself? Do you think it affects people's view of you?

_____

_____

_____

_____

_____

_____

_____

_____

_____

_____

_____

_____

_____

_____

Reflect

Based on your answers to the previous questions, what one thing are you willing to commit to that will feed your creative soul? Now think about it and use the space below to make a commitment to yourself. Just one small thing. You can do it! Come on!

I am ...

_____

_____

_____

_____

_____

_____

_____

_____

_____

Additional recommendations:

 Don't hate me here; I am going to make you work for your aural representation. Sit down for a few minutes and write out how you introduce yourself at work, at play, at a party. Now record yourself reading the introduction. When you listen to yourself, you will find places where maybe you hesitate, or places where you sound unsure or anxious. Repeat the writing part, fix the places you seemed to hesitate, then rerecord. Once you have the recording to your liking, start listening to it each day and start practicing it in public. Do you see a difference when you introduce yourself with your new story? This seemingly simple exercise is a powerful tool.

 Read *Rising Strong* by Brené Brown.

Read

FAILURE

I think I can write several books on this topic alone since I have failed so many times! I was speaking at a conference when an editor whom I admire a lot raised her hand and said, "Do you know what I like about you most? You are always talking about your failures."

Um. Yes.

I have failed many times. The first novel I wrote was possibly the worst piece of writing on this planet. I am on the ninth draft now, and still have a long way to go before it sees the light of day.[1]

---

[1] This essay was written a few years ago. My first novel, *Karma and the Art of Butter Chicken*, was published in September 2016. It stayed on the #1 Kindle list in Australia for three months. I have been blessed to have more than 20 sold-out events for the book. So the lesson of the story: YES, YOU CAN. I am working on the next novel now.

You must be wondering why I don't give up. What makes me want to go on to the tenth draft? Well, don't think I have not wanted to give up. There are days. But what I have learned is that when you are pursuing a dream that is a calling, not just a job, quitting is not an option.

But we have to be smart about it. I did quit a sci-fi type story I was trying to write because that was not where my heart was, and I recognized that it is not my strength as a writer.

I have decided that I will fail only when I stop trying. Until then, I keep on typing.

Please remind me of this when you see me whining on social media about how hard the tenth draft is to write!

Write

Your thoughts:

What sorts of situations have you faced that you deem a failure? What did you learn from them? In your mind, what is the difference between failing and giving up?

_____

_____

_____

_____

_____

_____

_____

_____

_____

_____

_____

_____

_____

_____

Reflect

Based on your answers to the previous questions, what one thing are you willing to commit to that will feed your creative soul? Now think about it and use the space below to make a commitment to yourself. Just one small thing. You can do it! Come on!

My failures …

_____

_____

_____

_____

_____

_____

_____

_____

Additional recommendations:

 There is a podcast called, I kid you not, *The Podcast of Doom*. Check it out and see if you learn something new about epic failures!

 I have read umpteen books on this subject. Some terrific ones are *Feel the Fear and Do It Anyway* by Susan Jeffers and *Failing Forward* by John C. Maxwell.

PROCRASTINATION

It is so ironic for me to write a post about procrastination, given that I have been looking for every excuse in the book to write this section later. Ah, I am the queen of procrastination. And it always surprises me. I mean, I gave up a life of financial security to become a writer, and what do I procrastinate about the most? Yep, writing.

When I first started writing, procrastination seemed glamorous. I would convince myself that I was not working because: The muse had not arrived; I just wasn't feeling the words; the sunrise was not dramatic enough; there weren't enough clouds in the sky. (You can see, no reason was really needed.)

Then it began to hurt my work. I found myself rushing on deadlines, having anxiety attacks over large stories, and in general chiding myself a lot over not writing.

One thing I have learned over the past ten years is that for art, any type of art, to be successful, the artist has to work diligently, regularly, consistently, and persistently. There is no other option.

As I am tempted to procrastinate on work now—and I am tempted quite often—I remind myself that this is a luxury I just cannot afford. If my art has even a small fighting chance of succeeding, I owe it to myself to work regularly on it.

I will say that this is still one of the harder battles I fight.

Write

Your thoughts:

Do you procrastinate? How do you deal with it? What are your tools to help you get over this?

_____

_____

_____

_____

_____

_____

_____

_____

_____

_____

_____

_____

_____

_____

Reflect

Based on your answers to the previous questions, what one thing are you willing to commit to that will feed your creative soul? Now think about it and use the space below to make a commitment to yourself. Just one small thing. You can do it! Come on!

I promise ...

_____

_____

_____

_____

_____

_____

_____

_____

Additional recommendations:

 Check out Tim Urban's TED Talk titled "**Inside the Mind of a Master Procrastinator.**"

 Read *The War of Art* by Steven Pressfield—an absolute must-read for creative minds!

REBIRTH

A couple of years ago, I was reading an interview of Grant Achatz and wondering what he would do next. (He is a fantastic chef who lost his sense of taste to cancer of the tongue.) A bit of Googling and I found out that his new restaurant would actually be called NEXT, a place where he and his team would be inventing and serving new menus every few months.

It is open now, and they are serving futuristic menus, classic menus—but the heart of it is that they are birthing it anew every three months: a creative rebirth in the true sense of the word. It strikes me as amazing. Such a simple idea, and yet one that will keep clients coming back for more new dishes. Creating an entire menu every three months is not for everyone, but therein is the point: It is for those of us whose professions are built on being creative.

This is such a critical lesson to learn as a creative person.

117

Inherent in the process of being an artist/entrepreneur of any kind is creative rebirth. This rebirth is what keeps our work fresh and keeps our ideas from an early grave.

Write

Your thoughts:

What does creative rebirth mean to you?

_____

_____

_____

_____

_____

_____

_____

_____

_____

_____

_____

_____

_____

_____

_____

Reflect

Based on your answers to the previous question, what one thing are you willing to commit to that will feed your creative soul? Now think about it and use the space below to make a commitment to yourself. Just one small thing. You can do it! Come on!

My creativity ...

_____

_____

_____

_____

_____

_____

_____

_____

_____

Additional recommendations:

 I know I have already recommended this, but please do listen to the *Invisibilia* podcast from NPR. It is terrific.

 Read books written by career changers. Also, I love *Who Moved My Cheese?* by Spencer Johnson and *What Color Is Your Parachute?* by Richard Nelson Bolles.

SADNESS

There are projects that die. No matter how talented the creator, how great the project, how awesome the reviews are, there are projects that do not make it. Books with great reviews sell only a few copies, paintings end up in Dumpsters, innovative products never make it to market. Why? I don't know. Maybe the timing wasn't right, maybe the stars did not align, maybe the artist wore the wrong shirt. What is my point? Shit happens.

I have had manuscripts shrivel up and die, and books that I thought would be awesome just barely create a flutter in the market. It is hard. As creative people, we put our heart and soul into our work, and when it doesn't succeed, all we want to do is quit.

I have created a coping technique to deal with the sadness that accompanies such a situation. I call it Timeboxed Whining.

Timeboxing is a technique I learned about during my

consulting days. Basically, it is a way to put a time limit around a situation. For instance, no matter what happens, the six o'clock news needs to go on at six. So the preparation work for that news needs a time box, which is to say it needs to be completed within a certain timeframe no matter what else happens because there is a hard deadline at the end.

Now, combine that with whining and you have a workable solution to mourning a failed project. This is a five-day exercise. (Artists swear by it. I do, too. It really works.) Here is how it works.

Days 1, 2, and 3: Set aside a time when you are going to whine. (Stay with me here.) I pick a time in the afternoon when I am prone to feeling sorry for myself and wondering how I will ever pull out of this failure. Set a timer for 15 minutes. Pull out a sheet of paper; no, you cannot do this on the computer. Now start writing all the reasons why you are upset and why the project failed and why you will never succeed again and why the whole world sucks. Instead of calling a friend and complaining about the economy/weather/whatever is bothering you and having them annoy you more(!), write it down. As Julia Cameron says, "Put the drama on the paper" where it belongs—and leave it there. Once your 15 minutes are up, place the paper in an envelope. You are not allowed to worry, whine, complain, or think about the project for any more time. Your time box is done.

Day 4: So now that you have finished the whining, move to the next step. Start the timer, but this time focus on all the lessons you have learned from this project. What did it teach you about your craft? About the market? About the audience for your product? Finish up and place this paper on your desk.

Day 5: Start the timer. Now write out what you would do again. What are the top three things about the project that totally rocked? What part did you love the most? At the end of the time, place this sheet on your desk and read it again and again. Take the envelope filled with the whining of the first three days and in a ritual that suits your temperament—burn it, rip it up and flush it down the toilet, place it in the recycling bin—do what you need to do to get rid of it.

It is gone. The sadness is out of your system. You have moved on. The papers in front of you are what it is about: what you have learned (Day 4) and how you will apply that to the next project (Day 5).

Now that you have uncluttered your mind of fears and worries, it is time to start working.

Write

Your thoughts:

How do you deal with the sadness of a failed project? What lessons have you learned? What is the one thing you can carry forward? What is the one thing you should not do again?

_____

_____

_____

_____

_____

_____

_____

_____

_____

_____

_____

_____

Reflect

Based on your answers to the previous questions, what one thing are you willing to commit to that will feed your creative soul? Now think about it and use the space below to make a commitment to yourself. Just one small thing. You can do it! Come on!

I promise ...

_____

_____

_____

_____

_____

_____

_____

_____

Additional recommendations:

 I am not going to recommend any podcast here. If you are dealing with a failed project, give yourself some time to recover. Listen to uplifting music, take walks, do whatever it takes to fill your creative well again and then—and this is key—let the failure go and move forward.

 You may enjoy *Resilience: Hard-Won Wisdom for Living a Better Life* by Eric Greitens, who was a Navy SEAL.

OVERTHINKING

I was seriously contemplating changing the name of my site to www.overthinking.com. Why? Because it is a skill that I feel I have honed and perfected.

It began innocently enough. I had a book of short stories that I sent to my agent in the hopes that he would try to sell them. *Now that it is in his hands*, I thought, *I can get going on my next piece of work.* This was a year ago. I started and stopped a million times as I tried to write a new novel. Nothing worked, nothing seemed right, and no matter what I did, I could not get started on my next piece of work.

Perhaps it was fear intruding: what if he cannot sell the stories? What if the editors hate them? Or worse—what if the stories sell and readers hate them?

Then the agent called: Short stories are hard to sell. No editor wants them.

That rejection was the final trigger: I essentially paralyzed my creative self.

I could write nothing of value, I decided, and so I quit the novel. Well, I quit writing it but not talking about it. I would whine about it each chance I got. To friends, strangers, people at the grocery store, my plants. A few are now dead as a result (plants, not people).

As I was cleaning my kitchen (which gleams when I am procrastinating), a friend stopped over to drop off something. She had heard me complain about this unwritten piece of work many, many, MANY times. Finally, in her most patient mom voice she said, "What if God's plan for you is to write a bad novel? Would you do it? Why not just write it? Why are you judging it? Why can't you trust your readers to judge it?"

She stopped me cold in my whining tracks.

A bad novel. I know I can write that. There is no pressure now, I thought.

I began to write. I emailed my writing buddy and said that soon she would have the first "shitty draft" to read. She responded, "You know—you are being a perfectionist. That is why you can't start anything on this book. Oh, and let's call it a rough draft, okay?"

Yes, a rough draft of a bad novel. I can do this.

Overcoming writer's block or resistance is hard. It comes in many forms and has many solutions. For me, the solution came in the form of my friend's sane advice: giving myself permission to fail. It is critical to the writing process, I would say to any creative process. I didn't feel like a sculptor who looks at a marble and sees a statue. I felt like a writer looking at the mirror and seeing a reflection of defeat. It was a hard feeling to shake off.

It has been a few weeks since my friend gave me that sane advice. I am writing. Peacefully, quietly, writing through the doubts, writing through the fears, writing through the rejections. Writing, creating art—constantly.

Write

Your thoughts:

What inspires you to create? Do you overthink things? What if you just let go for one day and created like you have nothing to lose? What would you create?

_____

_____

_____

_____

_____

_____

_____

_____

_____

_____

_____

_____

Reflect

Based on your answers to the previous questions, what one thing are you willing to commit to that will feed your creative soul? Now think about it and use the space below to make a commitment to yourself. Just one small thing. You can do it! Come on!

My inspiration ...

_____

_____

_____

_____

_____

_____

_____

_____

_____

Additional recommendations:

 If you are an overthinker like me, consider setting up a high-energy-songs playlist on an infinite loop to listen to when you start to feel the overthinking coming on. A great distraction for a while! Then, when you feel centered again, go back to creating.

 I am going to repeat a recommendation here: Steven Pressfield's *The War of Art*. A must-read.

GIVING UP

Last week, I made a rather harsh decision. I decided to quit writing. Forever.

To know how hard this decision was for me, consider this: All I have ever wanted to do is share stories. But sharing stories, in my culture, is the equivalent of being perpetually unemployable. So instead I earned myself an engineering degree with two masters in technology. And found myself employed with a six-figure job for more than a decade. But the calling to write was too strong, and in the end it won out. I became a writer, a food writer to be more specific. For the past several years, I wrote books, articles for national and international magazines and newspapers, and commentaries; got nominated for some awards; and even managed to get a syndicated column. I thought I had it made.

Until last week, that is.

You see, I met with a group of real writers. You know, the ones who, in my arena at least, went to cooking school, slaved for years in restaurant kitchens to pay for going to a top-of-the-line journalism school, started out in journalism by sorting mail, and eventually grew into editors, reporters, and award-winning writers. As I heard them speak about their experiences, I felt myself shrinking in size. Their chat made me realize my biggest fear: My writing could never ever be as rich as theirs, for I lacked the credentials they had. I thought I was a writer but after listening to them, I realized that I had no credentials to be a writer. I have never gone to culinary school, I have never stepped into the building of a journalism school, much less taken a college-level writing class.

I was what they were referring to as a fraud.

I walked home that night with a heavy heart. Here I was, over forty; should I consider going to cooking school? I already had several degrees that were "worth" several hundred thousand dollars, but they were totally worthless. Then I thought perhaps I should go and learn to write. I sat on the steps to my townhome and did something I haven't done since high school: I sat and wept. I don't know how long I was there, but probably for several hours.

When I got up to go into the house, I had made a decision. I was not going to write anymore. I couldn't.

The next morning, I stared at my computer. I had deadlines to meet, assignments that were due. I simply walked away. I could not bring myself to sit down and write anything. The inner critic had won. I had tuned in to his channel and bought his words hook, line, and sinker.

As the week progressed, I began to grow restless. I attributed it to lack of exercise and focus. I began to send resumes to make sure I could get something that looked and sounded like a real job to pay the bills. It made me even more restless.

Then, last night, I sat down and wrote in my dairy. I wrote like I have never written before. I wrote and wrote and wrote some more. As the words flowed, the restlessness began to disappear. As I filled the pages, my spirit lifted. As I searched for a different pen when I ran out of ink, I felt elated. The more I wrote, the freer I felt.

I realized what I had forgotten in listening to the real writers, and more so to my inner critic: True passion isn't about the end product of getting a byline. True passion is and will always be about the love of the process itself.

I subscribe to a newsletter called *Letters from the Universe*, and look at what popped into my email box: "The path to enlightenment is not a path at all, Monica, it's actually a metaphor for the time it takes for you to allow yourself to be happy with who you already are, where you're already at, and what you already have—no matter what."

So who am I? I am Monica Bhide and I am, on most days, a writer.

Write

Your thoughts:

Who are you? Why do you identify with that title/profession/label? What makes you you?

_____

_____

_____

_____

_____

_____

_____

_____

_____

_____

_____

_____

_____

_____

Reflect

Based on your answers to the previous questions, what one thing are you willing to commit to that will feed your creative soul? Now think about it and use the space below to make a commitment to yourself. Just one small thing. You can do it! Come on!

I am ...

_____

_____

_____

_____

_____

_____

_____

_____

_____

Additional recommendations:

 I highly recommend the *Unmistakable Creative* podcast.

 Read *Unmistakable: Why Only Is Better than Best* by Srinivas Rao—a wonderful book about finding and honoring your unique creative self.

BURDEN

I have changed some details in this story to conceal the identity of the person.

Years ago, I studied under a very charismatic but very difficult professor. He was the best in his field and super hard on his students. I was an A student but it was never enough. The A paper wasn't eloquent enough, the A test score wasn't perfect (huh?), the thesis was just not "shiny" (whatever that means). No matter what I did in his class, it was not good enough. That message really hit a nerve with me. I dreaded going to his classes and began skipping his lectures. I kept my grades by studying harder but avoided him in person.

While I was able to physically avoid him, his words had found a home in my brain and refused to leave. When I got my first job, I kept thinking that the paycheck would be better if I had been good enough. When I got my first promotion, I thought I would have received it earlier. I cannot tell you how many opportunities I passed up because my self-confidence was so low. To be fair to the professor, he was hard on everyone, and I do not blame him for what I did. I just took his words to heart and since I was already low on self-confidence, his words grew deep roots.

Fast-forward about twenty years. I am sitting at a café in town and I see him at the counter ordering coffee. I decide to go up and say hello. I am surprised at myself but I am no longer the engineer who wasn't good enough, I am now a published author, and I want to tell him that I have made something of my life.

"Hello, Doc," I say to him, and he looks at me as if I am an alien.

"I am Monica. I used to be one of your students at X college. . . ." His face is blank.

"My memory is fading. I remember teaching there but not much else."

I want to tell him so much, and here I am standing face-to-face with a very sad-looking old man.

"Oh, I have a question for you. When you were my student, was I nice to you?"

I know the answer to that one. I have been working on it all my life.

"Yes, Doc. You were."

His smile is feeble, there is no twinkle in his eyes, the charisma is long gone, the loud booming voice now trembles and whispers.

I shake his hand and leave.

I cried in the car. I cried for all the hate I had held for him. I cried that I took his words to heart. I cried at all that I had missed because of my own silliness of letting someone else's words define who I was.

As you follow your dreams, do not let this happen to you.

I beg you.

Your thoughts:

Have you let someone else define who you are or who you should be?
Think about it.

_____

_____

_____

_____

_____

_____

_____

_____

_____

_____

_____

_____

_____

Reflect

Based on your answers to the previous question, what one thing are you willing to commit to that will feed your creative soul? Now think about it and use the space below to make a commitment to yourself. Just one small thing. You can do it! Come on!

I let go ...

_____

_____

_____

_____

_____

_____

_____

_____

Additional recommendations:

If you could create your own podcast, what would it be? What topics would you choose? Why?

Read *You Are a Badass: How to Stop Doubting Your Greatness and Start Living an Awesome Life* by Jen Sincero.

CONTROL

Ah, this has got to be one of the topics I love to hate. Control: the myth that we can actually have power over anything except ourselves.

I remember when I started writing about food, my second career (after engineering), and I kept thinking that all I had to do was get published in some major publications and all would be great. I wrote a huge piece for *Gourmet* magazine, considered to be the topmost publication in food at the time. The editor decided to "kill" (not run) the story. I was furious. How could they do that? They said they loved it, paid me for it, and then chose not to run it. Lesson one in control: I don't have any control over what they do.

The lesson stays with me no matter what I take on—I can do what I can do, but I cannot control the results or other peoples' reactions, or make things go a certain way. All I can do is control myself, my words, my reactions, my thoughts.

It sounds so simple, right?

It is a very hard lesson to remember and execute when things do not go your way (which, by the way, will happen a lot when you set out to pursue a big dream). Things will fall apart, people will let you down, numbers will not go your way. This is the time to remember that all we can do is control our reactions and move onward and forward.

What other choice is there, really?

Write

Your thoughts:

What is it that you can control in yourself that will make you more creative?

_____

_____

_____

_____

_____

_____

_____

_____

_____

_____

_____

_____

_____

_____

Reflect

Based on your answers to the previous question, what one thing are you willing to commit to that will feed your creative soul? Now think about it and use the space below to make a commitment to yourself. Just one small thing. You can do it! Come on!

I commit ...

_____

_____

_____

_____

_____

_____

_____

_____

_____

Additional recommendations:

 Listen to *Happier with Gretchen Rubin.*

 Read *The Urban Monk* by Pedram Shojai.

ALL OR NOTHING

With all due respect, I think some people really should be careful what they write. (I include myself in that category, by the way.) I recently read in a piece by a motivational author that everyone who is serious about following their dreams should quit their day jobs. His argument was that if you do not quit your day job, how are you going to show your commitment to your dream?

Let me tell you: Please do not quit your day job unless your dream is in the phase where it is earning you a living that you are happy with, or you have money that can take care of you while you follow your dream.

Here is why. One of the first things that becomes difficult when you just quit one thing to do another—especially one that will not pay dividends instantly—is that you put yourself under serious financial pressure. It is very difficult to create something elegant, wonderful, and beautiful when you are worried about paying your mortgage, having enough to eat, or providing clothes for your kids.

Quitting your job to follow your dream doesn't show commitment, in my opinion. What shows commitment is finding the time and resources to apply toward your dream projects. As the dream projects take flight, then you can slowly let go of other things.

I quit my job to follow my dream. But I had a husband who was supporting me financially and emotionally and was coaching me throughout. Had it not been for him, I do not think I would have left the job to write. I would still have continued to write, but it would have been part-time until I could actually earn a living doing it.

Write

Your thoughts:

It is a difficult call. This is my opinion. What is yours? Is it all or nothing?

_____

_____

_____

_____

_____

_____

_____

_____

_____

_____

_____

_____

_____

_____

Reflect

Based on your answers to the previous questions, what one thing are you willing to commit to that will feed your creative soul? Now think about it and use the space below to make a commitment to yourself. Just one small thing. You can do it! Come on!

I will ...

_____

_____

_____

_____

_____

_____

_____

_____

_____

Additional recommendations:

 I love listening to podcasts when I go for my daily walk. One of my favorites is from Joanna Penn. I love her podcasts and her books. Do listen to her on *The Creative Penn*.

Read Joanna Penn's *How to Make a Living with Your Writing: Books, Blogging and More.* She has some other wonderful books for creative minds as well. Be sure to check out her website (thecreativepenn.com).

Read

FEEDBACK

No matter what your dream project is, at some point you will have to bring it in front of its intended audience. Whether it is a restaurant, a book, a flower shop, or an airplane (!), at the end of the day, it will be placed in front of, you know, *people*. And people, you gotta love them, will have an opinion. They may love it, hate it, not react to it, give you an award for it, or say they don't "get it."

Then what? Well, if you had asked me this when I first started working on my dream of becoming a writer, I would have told you that each word mattered. Each bit of feedback was critical. Each award was a much-needed feather in my cap.

Now, as I look back, can I just tell you that none of that really matters as much as we think it does? A good comment from a reader makes my day as much as a difficult critique from an admired editor makes me feel really bad. But at the end of the day, I have to take what I can and move on. Loving what I do and loving the process of doing it, I have realized, are much more important than focusing on the feedback at the end.

I am not saying that feedback is not important or that it cannot help us do better; what I am saying is that we need to keep it in perspective and not get hung up about it.

I was reading a blog post from a writer this morning about how let down he felt even after winning so many awards. Why? Because the world did not change the next day. If anything, he felt that the demands on him were higher, and he was wondering if he would let people down with his next work. Elizabeth Gilbert, the famed writer of *Eat, Pray, Love*, talks about this. I am paraphrasing here, but essentially her success with her first book terrified her and made her wonder if she could ever do it again. (For the record, she has, and in a wonderful way . . . by going back to doing what she loves and what is ultimately her passion: writing.)

An award is great and I will be happy if I get any or tons of them, but again, it is what it is. The next morning, I will still have to get up and face an empty page. And more importantly, I need to look forward to that empty page.

Write

Your thoughts:

As a creative person, how do you feel about feedback? Does it motivate you? Make you despair? What is the best way for YOU to deal with these reactions to feedback so that you can continue to create?

_____

_____

_____

_____

_____

_____

_____

_____

_____

_____

_____

_____

Reflect

Based on your answers to the previous questions, what one thing are you willing to commit to that will feed your creative soul? Now think about it and use the space below to make a commitment to yourself. Just one small thing. You can do it! Come on!

I commit ...

_____

_____

_____

_____

_____

_____

_____

_____

_____

Additional recommendations:

 Same recommendation here—listen to Joanna Penn's *Creative Penn* podcast.

 Read agent **Rachelle Gardner's blog**. She always has great advice for writers and other creative people on how to deal with rejection, feedback, etc.

GOOD ENOUGH?

Several years ago, I visited my older son's first grade class. There was a handwritten sign on one of the walls. A young child had written it, and it has stayed with me since that day. The sign read: "You are always telling me to do my best. I am trying. But what if my best is not good enough?"

I ponder this all the time. What if this piece I am writing is not good enough? What if my next book is not good enough? What if I do my best and it is not good enough?

The real question to me is: Who is judging?

I am my own worst critic so my opinion, in one sense, is immaterial. I have created a trusted group of advisors and I occasionally run things by them to see if the project in question is "good enough." Their feedback, which I trust, has helped me move forward on many occasions. Please remember that this is not random reader feedback; this is the feedback of people who understand and have experience in my industry.

And what if they say it is not good enough? Now that gives me choices (after I weep a few tears): I can learn how to fix it, I can decide to do nothing, I can move forward as is. The point is that now I am making an educated decision as to what is "good enough."

Write

Your thoughts:

What do you say? How perfect do things have to be to be "perfect"? Who decides on perfection?

_____

_____

_____

_____

_____

_____

_____

_____

_____

_____

_____

_____

_____

_____

Reflect

Based on your answers to the previous questions, what one thing are you willing to commit to that will feed your creative soul? Now think about it and use the space below to make a commitment to yourself. Just one small thing. You can do it! Come on!

I promise ...

_____

_____

_____

_____

_____

_____

_____

_____

Additional recommendations:

Creative Start is a good one to listen to! The podcast features interviews with writers, designers, bloggers, producers, dancers, and creative entrepreneurs about their journey to success.

Read Sarah Knight's wonderful satire *The Life-Changing Magic of Not Giving a F*ck: How to Stop Spending Time You Don't Have with People You Don't Like Doing Things You Don't Want to Do (A No F*cks Given Guide)*.

Read

EXCUSES

"I need an MFA," I explain, yet again, to my husband, who has asked why I'm not working on my novel, my dream project. Even as I mouth the words, I know I am exaggerating, as does he. It is my go-to excuse of the moment.

"You're a smart writer—why don't you just try to write and complete the novel instead of worrying about it so much?" he asks as gently as he can. I talk about the novel all the time. It is one of my biggest dreams. It has been in Draft One for about two years now. Maybe longer; I stopped counting. Yet I talk about it all the time. It doesn't let go.

He comes over and hugs me. "You know you can do this. Why are you so afraid?"

"You don't understand—writing a novel is different from all the narrative work I do now. I don't know how to build a character, I don't understand plotting, I have no idea how to create conflict for these characters—" I can feel my eyes brim with tears as I fight back the emotion that rears up at times like this, assuring me that I have failed.

He simply shakes his head. He knows I am stubborn. He leaves the room to avoid a scene and I turn to the TV.

I'm not much for watching reality TV, but the series that comes on catches my attention. It's a show based in India, and they are trying to find the "MasterChef" among competing home cooks. I know the judges and am instantly drawn to the show.

The novel is forgotten as I begin watching with interest. There are the usual suspects among the contestants: a housewife, a handsome young kid with a great desire to succeed, a cooking teacher, a caterer—but the one who catches my attention is a very young woman named Khoku. She is a servant in Delhi. Her day job is to go to people's homes and cook their meals. She and her family live in one of the tiniest rooms I have ever seen. The families she cooks for entered her into the contest because they felt her cooking was on a par with professional chefs. I watch her turn out dish after dish with ease, and listen in amazement as one of the top chefs in India, Sanjeev Kapoor, who has an audience of over 500 million (!) for his own shows, tells her that she should not be competing, but teaching chefs how to cook.

She is tiny, from what I can tell, and intense. While the others chat and look for attention, she seems uncomfortable in front of the camera. It is only when the camera catches her off guard that you see the personality. Her gaze is fixed on her work area, the cutting board, the knife. Occasionally you see her put an ingredient in her mouth and then close her eyes as she gives thought to its taste and texture. She seems to be in awe of where she is, just as the others are in awe of her raw talent.

Then come two challenges that change my view of my world, my own insecurities, and myself. First the contestants are to make pizza, Indian style. The judges hold up a pizza and tell the contestants that they must prepare one in a skillet (no oven) and it must have an Indian taste.

I see a strange look on Khoku's face that I am not able to decipher. And then it clicks: This young servant girl has never tasted pizza. Ever. The judges understand. Vikas Khanna, one of the judges and a top chef in New York City, walks over and hands her a slice so she knows what she is supposed to do. She passes that round with flying colors.

Next the contestants work with liquid nitrogen. They are given recipes that they must follow. I notice one of the judges standing with Khoku as she works. Another realization hits me: The girl does not know how to read or write. The judge is standing next to her to read her the recipe. Yet here she is, competing on a global stage next to the literate, the famous, the accomplished.

I look around at my table: I have stacks of books on writing novels. I have friends who are novelists and have offered to help. I have editors asking for the manuscript, and yes, I have the ability to read and write.

I think of Khoku: She simply relied on faith to carry her forward, without expectations.

The last show Khoku was on aired a couple of months ago. Since then I have started the second draft of my novel. I dusted off my books on the craft of fiction and began working through them. Each morning, before I begin, I think of her and her grace and her faith in her calling.

I have a long way to go, but this young woman taught me that faith in yourself is the first step in achieving your goals and your dreams. It occurred to me that my writing has never let me down, but by giving up, I was letting my craft down.

Write

Your thoughts:

Now tell me: What is your excuse for not moving forward on your dream project?

_____

_____

_____

_____

_____

_____

_____

_____

_____

_____

_____

_____

_____

Reflect

Based on your answers to the previous question, what one thing are you willing to commit to that will feed your creative soul? Now think about it and use the space below to make a commitment to yourself. Just one small thing. You can do it! Come on!

I will ...

Additional recommendations:

 I recommend *Happier with Gretchen Rubin*.

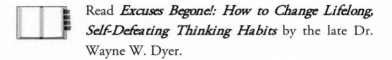 Read *Excuses Begone!: How to Change Lifelong, Self-Defeating Thinking Habits* by the late Dr. Wayne W. Dyer.

FAITH AND FORTUNE

A few years ago, a dear friend told me to buy a book called *A Fortune-Teller Told Me*. It is a book about a jet-setting reporter, Tiziano Terzani, who was advised by an Asian fortune-teller not to fly for a year or he would surely die. The reporter was told that he had to do all his traveling by car or train or boat. Instead of ignoring the fortune-teller, the author embraced the prediction. He did not fly and chose to do his work by crisscrossing Asia without ever setting foot off solid ground. Then, of course, predictably, he wrote a book about his adventures.

I enjoyed the book. It is a very interesting read.

But something about the fortune-teller stayed with me.

I kept thinking about all the "fortune-tellers" in my own life. I have had people tell me all kinds of things, ranging from "you are going to be a complete disaster as a writer" to "you are going to win amazing awards for your writing." The people who make these predictions are not psychic or gifted astrologers, but rather they are people who genuinely care about me and my well-being.

Whether I like it or not, they are my personal fortune-tellers.

So the question arises, whom should I listen to? The gloom-and-doom teller or the all-things-are-glorious teller?

I happen to think both are wrong, but in my heart of hearts I worry—what if they are not? Should I go back to my day job? Should I start clearing shelves to hold all the awards I am going to win?

It is very hard to not let other people define who we are and who we want to be. The author of the book I mentioned above was one of the lucky few. The prediction he received helped him. Most don't. They are exactly the opposite; they are truly detrimental to success. At least that is what I feel. Let's say I take the gloomy prediction about my career seriously. Then I have done myself a disservice by not even trying. And if I take the glorious prediction, then I am setting myself up for having my hopes and expectations crushed if the fortune-teller is wrong.

The only one who can predict the future is: NO ONE.

Many smart and savvy people can predict what could *possibly* happen, but with 100 percent certainty? No way.

We have to live with these fortune-tellers, but not with their prophecies. We have to learn to live in the realm of possibility, of hope, of faith. We have to create our own fortunes.

I was thinking about this as I was driving this morning. I stopped at a light and read the sticker on the car in front of me: "True faith will always be rewarded." Now that is the fortune you can take to the bank.

Write

Your thoughts:

Do you believe that the people who are predicting your failure (or success) are correct? Why do you believe them? Do you believe you will fail or succeed? Whose opinion matters more: yours or theirs?

Reflect

Based on your answers to the previous questions, what one thing are you willing to commit to that will feed your creative soul? Now think about it and use the space below to make a commitment to yourself. Just one small thing. You can do it! Come on!

My fortune ...

_____

_____

_____

_____

_____

_____

_____

_____

Additional recommendations:

 There are some very interesting podcasts that talk about the future (through the eyes of technology, etc.). If you feel so inclined, I would encourage you to listen to those and see what you can glean from them to help your creative side. The *Review the Future* podcast is a good one to start with.

 Read *A Fortune-Teller Told Me* by Tiziano Terzani (of course this is the book I would recommend!).

Read

SURROUND YOURSELF WITH PASSIONATE PEOPLE

I surround myself with friends who wear their passions, their dramas, on their sleeves, and regale me with stories of the exotic, the experiential, the practical, and the mystical. They are always "on fire."

Let me introduce you to my friend Jim. He used to hold a high-profile position in the Defense Department and now works for a private firm offering creative business solutions to clients. He is one of those people who frequently tell "I caught a fish this big" stories, with one big difference: his stories are all true. Whether he's been in Baghdad or Philadelphia, when he talks, his stories command attention. His larger-than-life stories are told with the eagerness of a curious child. More than anything else, though, what attracts me to his stories is the passion with which he tells them. Here is a man who has the right to be jaded, and maybe should be, based on all the horrific scenes he has witnessed in war-torn zones around the world. Yet he isn't. His curiosity about life is contagious.

"I want to travel to Australia and spend time with this tribe on this remote island," he tells me. Why? It has nothing to do with what he does at work. "The world is so big, there is so much to learn. I want to be out there learning. How do they do what they do? Can it help us? How does biology help us? How does physics? I want to be out there and learn. You never know what a tribe is doing well that could help us deal with the problem of eradicating a disease or hunger or . . . I want to learn." And that he does, occasionally running away to Japan, or to Arizona to study the border patrol solution and learn how to apply those principles in other areas. One evening with Jim and you want to fly to the Himalayas and see what it takes to climb them, or to Vegas and see how the Bellagio really runs—he just has a lust for life and its adventures.

If I need the history of anything, I listen to my friend Rami. Janet has taught me how to enjoy nature by learning about the leaves, flowers, and little creatures that inhabit our neighborhood. My friend Nazu, a writer, spends her free time as a clown doctor; her stories always teach me humility. All of these friends have full-time jobs, but that is not what defines them; what sets them apart is their passion—this is what makes them different. Their varied ethnicities and backgrounds lend completely different flavors and seasonings to their tales. Their ardent fervor for life lifts my spirits and refills my creative reservoir with wonderment. They are not all Pollyannas, but they do all have positive energy that I find uplifting.

It's true that just one conversation with any of these people results in the birth of innumerable ideas. More importantly, it reignites my own passion for my work.

Write

Your thoughts:

Who are some of the passionate people in your life? What makes them tick? What have you learned from them?

_____

_____

_____

_____

_____

_____

_____

_____

_____

_____

_____

_____

_____

_____

Reflect

Based on your answers to the previous questions, what one thing are you willing to commit to that will feed your creative soul? Now think about it and use the space below to make a commitment to yourself. Just one small thing. You can do it! Come on!

My tribe ...

_____

_____

_____

_____

_____

_____

_____

_____

Additional recommendations:

 I highly recommend *Dear Sugar Radio* and *Dear Sugars*, hosted by Cheryl Strayed and Steve Almond.

 Read *Wild: From Lost to Found on the Pacific Crest Trail* by Cheryl Strayed.

LEARN

Earlier this year I took a class on how to be a psychic. I am working on a fictional story where the lead character is a medium and I wanted to learn the lingo. Next week, I am taking a class on travel writing. Ah, you think I am showing off how much I am willing to learn? On the contrary, I am telling you how little I know!

When I first embarked on my new dream career, I knew there was a lot I needed to learn, as I did not even know the basics. Once I learned the basics, I thought, I would be on my way. But I would not dream of a taking a writing class or learning anything new. (I had several degrees under my belt, and my thought was that I was done with learning.)

I don't think I could have been more wrong if I'd tried. As I began to tackle the more difficult aspects of writing, I began to realize how little I knew about writing—or about much else. I recall in my earlier days working on a piece about mushrooms and being ashamed of how little I knew about them. Then I worked on story about sake and realized that I knew even less about sake than I did about mushrooms.

I now routinely take classes, read more books than I ever have before, ask a lot of questions, and no longer attempt to hide my ignorance. It helps me be creative and keep the passion for learning alive.

Write

Your thoughts:

If we stop learning, how will we grow? What one new thing will you learn this month? There are so many free classes on the internet, will you sign up for something that is totally new to you?

_____

_____

_____

_____

_____

_____

_____

_____

_____

_____

_____

Reflect

Based on your answers to the previous questions, what one thing are you willing to commit to that will feed your creative soul? Now think about it and use the space below to make a commitment to yourself. Just one small thing. You can do it! Come on!

I promise ...

_____

_____

_____

_____

_____

_____

_____

_____

_____

Additional recommendations:

 No audio assignment for this one!

This reading assignment is actually more of a research assignment. Find classes in your area of interest and pick one that you will take. There is so much free on the internet, so I am not asking you to spend money here. **HarvardX** offers a boatload of free online courses. Or check out **Udemy** or **Coursera**; both offer paid courses, but occasionally they offer some good discounts.

ENRICH YOUR LIFE

If you have ever heard me speak at an event or have taken any of my classes, you will know that I am very partial to Pink Floyd, in particular these lyrics: "All you touch and all you see, is all your life will ever be." I love them so much that I have a T-shirt with these lines.

I don't think anything can be truer than these lyrics when it comes to enriching our lives. The more we learn, the more we see, the more we understand the world around us. In fact, I remember years ago my grandmother used to say that if you are bored with life, change the sky that you see. She meant travel around and learn. There is so much we don't know, so much we assume, so much to learn. Travel doesn't have to take us to exotic lands (although, I have to admit, that is fun) but can just be to a new little city around the corner, to the mountains, to the lakes nearby—anything that helps shift perspective.

I like to read a lot, but I used to find myself reading the same types of books—spy thrillers or medical thrillers. I loved them and especially loved reading a lot of trashy novels. So I made a deal with myself: For every book I read that was trashy, I would read one that I would never have picked. I asked people for recommendations and read books I would not normally touch—books on malaria, a book on the origin of color, a book on understanding the science behind intentions. I find myself more and more curious about life after reading these and, can I tell you, it keeps me humble and makes me realize how little I know.

Write

Your thoughts:

What new thing is on your list to do? "All you touch and all you see, is all your life will ever be ..." as Pink Floyd says!

_____

_____

_____

_____

_____

_____

_____

_____

_____

_____

_____

_____

_____

Reflect

Based on your answers to the previous question, what one thing are you willing to commit to that will feed your creative soul? Now think about it and use the space below to make a commitment to yourself. Just one small thing. You can do it! Come on!

My list ...

_____

_____

_____

_____

_____

_____

_____

_____

Additional recommendations:

 Pick a podcast that focuses on a totally contrary view of a topic you love. Listen to at least two episodes. What did you learn?

 Read a book that you would never, ever, under any circumstances be caught dead reading. Yep— THAT BOOK! Read it. What did you learn?

BE GRATEFUL

I was about seven when a young, newlywed, gorgeous Indian woman with a serious UK accent invited me to her house for a "special celebration." It did not sound tempting till she told me I could not only bring friends but that she would serve my favorite foods.

A few days after accepting this lunch invitation, six of the nosiest, giggliest girls you would ever meet showed up at her house. Barely had we stepped in when we were asked to remove our slippers and then move onto a large balcony. There, her husband, an eye surgeon, came out with a large steel pitcher in his hand and then began to wash our feet. I was mortified. My friends did not seem to care as they giggled and wiggled. Not me. Was he implying we were unclean?

The lady noticed. "Come, Monica, let me dry your feet and then we will eat." I could smell the toasty cumin and hear the sizzle of the bread frying in the wok. It smelled good enough to forgive her husband's thoughtless task. She used a small towel to dry off my wet feet.

We were then asked to sit in a circle and she began to hand out presents—a dozen red bangles, a red stole, and a silver coin. We were restless as she tried to explain the reason for the gifts and the significance of each thing. Where was the wonderful food that we could smell?

She must have sensed it. She went into the kitchen and came back with tiny silver platters filled with black chickpea curry redolent of cinnamon and cloves, golden semolina pudding dotted with sweet raisins and crunchy cashews, deep-fried balloon bread scented with cumin, lentil wafers, a mild homemade mango pickle, and even a bowl of sweetened yogurt. As we ate the hearty and nourishing meal, she began to tell us a story about *Kanjaks*. Our group pretended to pay attention as we gobbled as much as our little mouths could hold. Kanjaks— young prepubescent girls—are revered in various parts of India as incarnates of Goddess. Girls are the very essence of purity and bliss, she said. The washing of the feet, the giving of the gifts, feeding us such a lavish meal—we were being treated like goddesses, she said.

Recently I was reminiscing with my mother about how great this lady's food used to be. My mother turned to me, surprised that I had not understood the real meaning of what her friend had been trying to do. In India, where killing a female fetus was considered "normal" and boys were thought of as the more desirable offspring, she was reviving this age-old tradition to give little girls like me true self-esteem. To ensure, I think, in her own way, that when these Kanjaks grew up, they had the same pride about bearing daughters as they did sons.

And I thought I was there for the food.

Write

Your thoughts:

What are you grateful about? Do you remember any gratitude rituals from when you were a child? Do you still practice them? If you had to create a new gratitude ritual, what would it be?

_____

_____

_____

_____

_____

_____

_____

_____

_____

_____

_____

_____

Reflect

Based on your answers to the previous questions, what one thing are you willing to commit to that will feed your creative soul? Now think about it and use the space below to make a commitment to yourself. Just one small thing. You can do it! Come on!

My gratitude ritual ...

_____

_____

_____

_____

_____

_____

_____

_____

_____

Additional recommendations:

 Gratitude & Trust podcast by Tracey Jackson and Paul Williams. They don't have new episodes but the old ones are worth listening to. The podcast features interviews with Patricia Cornwell, Rosanne Cash, Margaret Atwood, Martha Stewart, and many others.

 Read *Gratitude & Trust* by Tracey Jackson and Paul Williams.

GRACE

"Oh, this has high-fructose corn syrup in it, I don't think I can eat this," remarked a business associate when I presented her with some beautifully packaged homemade peanut brittle that I had purchased from a woman who had just started her own brittle-making business. At first, I was taken aback by the reaction. But then I was just annoyed—it was a gift. She could have taken it, said thank you, and then thrown it in the trash when I left; that would have been gracious. But no, she made a point to turn the package around, read the ingredients list on the back and then scrunch her face and make a rude remark. (And no, she is not allergic to corn syrup.)

Webster's defines *graciousness* as being good and courteous, and to a point I agree, but I think there is so much more to it. Graciousness brings with it a certain polish, a charm that touches us. Gracious people are not just polite and kind—they share an attitude that spreads abundance of a positive spirit. Let me give you an example (or two).

When I lived in Cleveland, Ohio, several years ago, my husband and some friends and I went to a restaurant downtown for dinner. As we were waiting to enter the restaurant, it began to thunder, and rain looked imminent. A kind, tall, and very handsome gentleman who was ahead of us in line to get in stopped, opened the door and held it for all of us to go in first, and said, "Please, come on in." We smiled at him and entered. It was kind, you say? Polite? The man holding the door was a superstar, a renowned basketball player. We had no idea who he was until he entered the restaurant and heads turned.

Which brings me to my second example—I grew up in the Bahrain, one of the most hospitable places in the world (nothing like what has been shown on TV in 2015). I must have been about 16 when my parents, my sister, and I were invited to a dinner at a friend's home on a Thursday night. So we showed up at seven with hostess gift in hand. "I don't see too many cars outside," my dad commented. "I guess it is a small gathering." When the hostess opened the door, wearing sweats, we knew instantly we had made a mistake in the date. Totally embarrassed, my ever-polite and gentle father said, "I am so very sorry, we thought the dinner was tonight." To which the hostess smiled and said, "It is now. We are blessed that you have been sent our way this day. Come in and we will celebrate being together and eat whatever I can get out of the fridge." It was one of the best evenings of our lives. Her graciousness touched me in so many ways—if her reaction had been merely polite, it could have made us feel like fools. As we were getting ready to leave, she thanked my mother warmly for the flowers we had brought. "You don't need to bring a gift when you come, just your friendship is gift enough," she said.

I end with these words that someone wrote in my memory book in high school. I don't know if he is the original author of these lines or if he borrowed them from somewhere. So with all due respect to the author of these lines, here you go: "Be a gracious person, for graciousness is a charm, that no friend can ever borrow and no foe can ever harm."

Write

Your thoughts:

Have you seen someone being less than gracious? What has that taught you? Would you like to be more gracious? What is the one thing you can do today to be more gracious?

_____

_____

_____

_____

_____

_____

_____

_____

_____

_____

_____

_____

_____

_____

Reflect

Based on your answers to the previous questions, what one thing are you willing to commit to that will feed your creative soul? Now think about it and use the space below to make a commitment to yourself. Just one small thing. You can do it! Come on!

I commit ...

_____

_____

_____

_____

_____

_____

_____

_____

_____

Additional recommendations:

I have searched in vain but cannot find a good podcast on the art of grace! Perhaps this is a podcast that needs to be created! Any takers?

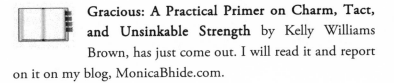

Gracious: A Practical Primer on Charm, Tact, and Unsinkable Strength by Kelly Williams Brown, has just come out. I will read it and report on it on my blog, MonicaBhide.com.

Read

BE PRESENT

One afternoon, I was checking my email, watching the pot as curry simmered, picking up after my baby, mentally making a list of all that needed to be done that afternoon, and pretending to listen to my eight-year-old son who was reciting me a poem for Mother's Day. Suddenly, my ever-polite child yelled rudely, "Mama, where are you? We are here . . . where are you?"

I stopped what I was doing and turned to my son. All of a sudden, everything around me seemed to slow down. His simple question had stumped me. I was everywhere but where I needed to be. I was working around them and for them but not there in spirit with my kids.

I went to my office, where I had placed a quote by Deepak Chopra on the wall.

Living in the present moment creates the experience of eternity. It is like every drop of water in an ocean contains the flavor of the whole ocean. So too, every moment in time contains the flavor of eternity, if you could live in that moment, but most people do not live in the moment, which is the only time they really have. They either live in the past or the future. If you could live in the moment, you would see the flavor of eternity and when you metabolize the experience of eternity, your body doesn't age.

It clicked, finally. The author's entire message clicked. And it caught me off guard. I had always read any inspirational book I could get my hands on—Deepak Chopra, Pema Chodron, Wayne Dyer, and so many more. I would find that I always felt good while reading the books and then once I put them down, I would begin to feel anxious again. I never implemented their suggestions. It always felt like another thing to add to my to-do list, and if I am honest, I never felt I could meditate. My mind ran in 19 directions all at once and I did not have the strength, or so I felt, to quiet it down. The books promised a land of peace, and I was scared—what if I tried and didn't find it? They provided an illusion that perhaps someday I too could be peaceful like them. I had chosen to not even try.

As I looked around the room and at my kids, I realized I was doing a lot of "good parenting" but not really being there for them. I took great care of them, but what I needed to do was be present with them when I was with them and shut down the electronic world, my future worry lists, my past holdups, and anything else.

I sat down feeling drained and then strangely relieved. I am a strong believer in the saying that when the student is ready, the teacher appears.

Chopra's message helped me change my attitude and made me, and those around me, a lot happier. It began with smaller things. I decided not to give myself a hard time about meditation and instead began to simply focus on breathing. I wake up each morning and spend 20 minutes on focused breathing. I go out for "centering" walks sometimes and focus on nature—no iPhones, cell phones, iTunes, or any tunes. At least once every few hours, I remind myself to breathe. Sounds simplistic? It has made a world of difference. It is amazing how shallow my breaths were and now how much less tense my body is.

Today, as I write this, I am sitting at my dining table in my townhome in Virginia. I am staring out the gorgeous floor-to-ceiling windows that overlook a garden with vividly colored flowers and a spectacularly blue sky with a sprinkling of a cloud or two.

Write

Your thoughts:

Today, I try to make sure that I am present in my own life. Are you?

_____

_____

_____

_____

_____

_____

_____

_____

_____

_____

_____

_____

_____

_____

_____

Reflect

Based on your answers to the previous question, what one thing are you willing to commit to that will feed your creative soul? Now think about it and use the space below to make a commitment to yourself. Just one small thing. You can do it! Come on!

I am ...

_____

_____

_____

_____

_____

_____

_____

_____

Additional recommendations:

 On Being is really a wonderful podcast by Krista Tippett.

 Read *The Power of Now* by Eckhart Tolle—a wonderful, life-changing book.

TAKE A DIFFERENT
PERSPECTIVE

Nine times out of ten, I find that my students give up on a project because after the nth time trying to make it work/trying to make it perfect/trying to make it educational/trying to make it creative, they are faced with the worst realization a creative person can ever face: What they have created is boring. I run into this in my own writing and just hate when that happens. Everything seems to read the same way, all the references appear recycled, all my innovative ideas seem like they are from a time when Adam met Eve.

So what do I do when this happens? A technique that I have found very helpful (but only after I cry into my coffee for a while) is to change perspectives on what is being done. For instance, if I am writing a story about the use of spices for an audience over age 50, I redo the story and see what happens if I target that same piece for a group of five-year-olds. (This, by the way, is a true example.) If I am working on a piece about fear of flying—which I have been trying to overcome for years—I look to stories not just about overcoming fear but about what happens to those who don't. Changing how you look at something can really alter the way you define it.

Here is another example. In our house (I think I am going to send the kids into therapy for this), here is how colors pair up:

As red as rice
As white as eggplant
As purple as cauliflower
As black as a carrot

The kids use these as references because it is what they see most often. I could never have done this, since I did not know about any of these growing up. My rice was white, my eggplant purple, my cauliflower cream-colored, and my carrot orange.

Write

Your thoughts:

This is critical to making something that seems boring more exciting: Look at something very familiar from a different point of view. As you go through your day, refocus on the familiar. What new things are you noticing?

_____

_____

_____

_____

_____

_____

_____

_____

_____

_____

_____

Reflect

Based on your answers to the previous question, what one thing are you willing to commit to that will feed your creative soul? Now think about it and use the space below to make a commitment to yourself. Just one small thing. You can do it! Come on!

My new perspective ...

_____

_____

_____

_____

_____

_____

_____

_____

_____

Additional recommendations:

 The perfect podcast for this is, hands down, *Invisibilia* from NPR. The entire focus of the podcast is to help us widen our perspectives! Highly recommend!

 Since this entire book is about changing perspective, I am not going to add another one here for now!

Read

COMMIT

When I was in the midst of trying to sell my narrative book proposal, I was terribly frustrated. Nothing was going the way that I wanted and I kept looking back at the (now seemingly) wonderful job I had left behind to become a writer. The frustration had begun to take over from the dream.

It was at this point that I met Chris Dorris. His focus is providing mental toughness training for everyone from CEOs to athletes. I called him to ask what I was doing wrong and why I was getting so frustrated. He taught me about the concept of **ALL IN**.

> *When we are fully committed to something—and I mean FULLY—we are at our most powerful. When we are infinitely committed, the possibility of not doesn't appear on our radar or doesn't exist within our consciousness. So*

our actions are as masterful as they can be. Infinite commitment is what I mean by the term, ALL IN! And it's a state of mind. Just like anxiety is a state of mind. Or confidence. Or hopelessness. No human state of mind is as powerful and useful as the knowing, or ALL IN state. And every state is a choice, so I recommend choosing ALL IN!

He went on to talk to me about the fact that I was always looking back at what could have been; instead of looking at my obstacles as easily surmountable, I was looking at them as excuses and wondering about my decision to leave my job and become an independent writer. It sounds simple enough but it hit me like a ton of bricks. In my heart, I wasn't 100 percent committed. I had a lot of what-ifs that I worried about. I had a lot of anxiety. Instead of using my energy to further myself as a writer, I was using it to worry about my future—which, if you haven't guessed by now, is a total waste of time.

Chris helped me refocus my energy and commit to my work and be ALL IN.

Write

Your thoughts:

Are you committed to your dream project? Are you ALL IN? This questions holds whether you are a full-time or a part-time creative entrepreneur. The point is to be fully committed when you are dedicating yourself to something and not let doubt seep in.

_____

_____

_____

_____

_____

_____

_____

_____

_____

_____

_____

Reflect

Based on your answers to the previous questions, what one thing are you willing to commit to that will feed your creative soul? Now think about it and use the space below to make a commitment to yourself. Just one small thing. You can do it! Come on!

I commit ...

_____

_____

_____

_____

_____

_____

_____

_____

_____

Additional recommendations:

 Check out Chris Dorris on YouTube taking about Creating Your Dream.

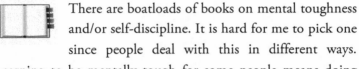 There are boatloads of books on mental toughness and/or self-discipline. It is hard for me to pick one since people deal with this in different ways. Learning to be mentally tough for some people means doing more yoga, or meditating; for others it can be rigorous physical training or attending workshops with career coaches. You have to pick the right style for yourself. That said, *I Am Malala* by Malala Yousafzai is a good one to start with—a great case study in the strength of the human spirit.

HOPE

As I write this last essay, my husband is recovering from a massive stroke, I have survived a nasty car accident, and a very dear one has called to tell me that cancer has struck. To say that it feels like I am rearranging the deck chairs on the *Titanic* would be an understatement. And yet, here I am, writing.

During this time of hardship, I find myself reaching again and again for the only thing that gives me great comfort: books. For some people, it is music, or medication, or meditation, or walking, or yoga, or rock climbing. For me, it is and always will be books. I have found myself reading everything from old favorites, such as *When Breath Becomes Air*, to contemporary releases like *Into the Water* by Paula Hawkins. I read books about my husband's illness, about finding motivation during hard times, about how to care for yourself while caring for others. During endless hours in waiting rooms, I read what felt like every magazine available. (I'm now completely updated on George Clooney's twins.)

As the political climate got nastier, I found myself researching old books about what all this means. What happened during the time of Nixon, and is there any parallel? Earlier in the election cycle, there was a lot of discussion about the daily security briefing a president receives; I wondered what that was all about, and how and why it was done. Yes—there was a book on it. I remember ordering it and learning more on a topic that has nothing to do with what I do for a living; but it helped me understand what the issues being spoken about really mean.

I wrote a blog post years ago, wondering if my current profession—food writing—even matters. The variety of responses surprised me then. But nothing surprised me more than what happened when massive tragedy hit home. I wasn't able to cook or feed my family as I wanted—but I found myself, late at night, reaching for the cookbooks on my nightstand. Just going through them comforted me, provided solace, and made me think of happier times. I began to bookmark recipes I would cook when things settled down. They gave me hope . . . that things *would* settle down.

All this made me wonder: What if, during hard times—whether personal, professional, or political—we writers stopped writing? What if painters stopped painting? What if photographers stopped taking pictures? I say this because that was my first instinct when my whole world fell apart: I stopped writing. My friends, my mentor, and my father constantly told me to keep a journal, but at first I scoffed. How could they tell me to keep writing when everything seemed to be going up in flames? And then, slowly, I realized what was giving me comfort was *words*. Words others had written during times of great turmoil. And some not written during times of turmoil. But all those words offered me great relief during a heartbreaking time. Getting lost in a good mystery to avoid dealing with medical what-ifs for an hour was a blessing. Even if just for an hour.

What if no one had documented diseases, plagues, wars, personal illnesses? We would lose who we are as humanity.

It is easy to write during good times—and we must do so. Telling stories of success, of overcoming hardship, is important. Funny movies, inspiring songs, great photographs lift us all no matter what our environment is.

I hope this book has inspired you to create your art from your heart and your gut. Write freely, paint with abandon, don't let the obstacles (big, small, or otherwise) dictate who you should be. You are in control of yourself and your work no matter what the circumstances. This is a lesson I have learned over and over again. Everything comes from within me. It is all that I can control. I cannot control what is outside me. I can, however, control what I choose to release in this world. What is it that you want to release into this world? What will be your legacy? What art/creative initiative will you leave behind after you are gone? How do you want people to remember you and your work?

I ask this of you as much as I ask this of myself.

I hope as you and I explore this world we are in, with all its wonders and its flaws, we will write and create art as much as we can, so someday our future generations will have the books/paintings/photographs/words/illustrations/movies that give them pleasure in their time of peace and solace in their time of need.

Reflect

I hope you have enjoyed this book. Tell me what this book has taught you. Did any particular stories hit home? Did any topic really resonate?

I would also love for you to use these pages to tell your own story. *Where are you going from here?*

_____

_____

_____

_____

_____

_____

_____

_____

_____

_____

_____

About Monica Bhide

Monica Bhide is an internationally renowned writer known for sharing food, culture, mystery, love, and life in a lyrical voice. Having roots and experience in many places, Monica is now based in the Washington, DC area. She has built a diverse and solid audience through the publication of three cookbooks, a book of essays and one of short stories, a collection of interviews with exceptional women in food, her website, *MonicaBhide.com*, and articles in top-tier media including *Food & Wine*, *Bon Appétit*, *Saveur*, *The Washington Post*, *Health*, the *New York Times*, *Ladies Home Journal*, *AARP The Magazine*, and *Parents*. Her books have been published by Simon & Schuster and Random House (India). Monica released her debut short story collection, *The Devil in Us*, in October 2014. Her sixth book, *A Life of Spice*, a collection of food essays, was released on April 27, 2015. *Karma and the Art of Butter Chicken*, Monica's first novel, was released on September 1, 2016.

An engaging storyteller, informed educator, and popular lecturer, Monica has taught writing and social media workshops around the world, at Food Bloggers Connect (London),

Association of Food Journalists (Salt Lake City), Eat Write Retreat (DC and Philadelphia), Food and Wine Conference (Orlando), Georgetown University and Yale University (as a guest speaker), and elsewhere. She frequently teaches writing classes for Smithsonian Associates in Washington, DC. Monica is also a frequent presence on NPR.

Monica has given keynote speeches at various organizations for the past several years. Her topics have included finding your creative self and renewing your creative strength in an ever-changing world.

Monica's food writing has garnered numerous accolades and been included in four *Best Food Writing* anthologies (2005, 2009, 2010, and 2014). The *Chicago Tribune* named her one of seven food writers to watch in 2012. In April 2012, *Mashable.com* picked her as one of the top ten food writers on Twitter.

Monica is a graduate of The George Washington University, Washington, DC. She holds a master's degree from Lynchburg College, Lynchburg, VA, and a bachelor's degree from Bangalore University in Bangalore, India. She feels fortunate for her rich education and enjoys giving back to the global community by serving on committees and volunteering for Les Dames d' Escoffier, the International Association of Culinary Professionals, and other organizations.

About Simi Jois

Simi uses photographic images as her canvas and the lens as her brush. Her passion for creating flavors in the kitchen provided her with infinite permutations of expression. Painting with ingredients, pairing exotic spices for mutual enhancement and richness of flavor, Simi narrates her stories through the play of light and bold strokes of color.

Simi's portfolio: http://www.simijois.com
Simi's blog: http://www.turmericnspice.com

Acknowledgments

I want to thank my family and dear friends who encourage me and my crazy dreams. A special thanks to my husband, Sameer Bhide, for keeping me motivated!

Thanks to Casey Benedict, who inspired me to create Powered by Hope and guided me through its execution.

Simi Jois reminds me every day what it means to be surrounded by supportive, talented, and passionate friends.

A big shout-out to Marcia Turner, who curated the content for me from my yearlong project. Thank you to Suzanne Fass, Jason Anderson, and James aka Humble Nations for all their hard work on editing, designing, and cover design of this book. Big hugs and thanks to my amazing muses who have kept me on the straight and narrow: Stephanie Caruso, Paayal Sharma, Luca Marchiori, Popsy Kanagaratnam, Betty Ann Besa-Quirino, Ana Di, Amy Riolo, Niv Mani, Aviva Goldfarb, Mollie Cox Bryan, Linda Whittig, and Ramin Ganeshram, Britt Jackman, and Ana Borray, thank you!!

This book is dedicated to my children, Jai and Arjun, for inspiring me to always think outside the box.

Also by Monica Bhide

Inspirational Books

In Conversation with Exceptional Women (ebook)

Fiction and Short Stories

Karma and the Art of Butter Chicken (Bodes Well Publishing, 2016)

The Devil in Us (2014)

Mother (Bodes Well Publishing, 2018)

The Soul Catcher (Bodes Well Publishing, 2018)

Poetry

Telltales (Bodes Well Publishing 2017)

Food Essays and Cookbooks

A Life of Spice (2015)

Modern Spice: Inspired Indian Flavors for the Contemporary Kitchen (Simon and Schuster, 2009; Random House India, 2010)

The Everything Indian Cookbook: 300 Tantalizing Recipes from Sizzling Tandoor Chicken to Fiery Lamb Vindaloo (Adams Media, 2004)

Monica's essays have been included in *Best Food Writing 2005, 2009, 2010,* and *2014,* edited by Holly Hughes (Da Capo Press)

Monica's books are available through Amazon.com, BN.com, Kobo, iBooks and her website, MonicaBhide.com. Please connect with me at monicabhide.com for news, free books, events and more

Made in the USA
Middletown, DE
07 February 2024